Due Return Date Date	Due Return Date Date

The Documentary Sources of Greek History

The
Documentary Sources
of Greek History

By M. CARY

GREENWOOD PRESS, PUBLISHERS
NEW YORK

Originally published in 1927 by, and reprinted
with the permission of Basil Blackwell

First Greenwood Reprinting 1969

Library of Congress Catalogue Card Number 78-90478

SBN 8371-2215-5

PRINTED IN UNITED STATES OF AMERICA

PREFACE

THE object of this book is to serve as an introduction to the study of Greek historical documents. It seeks to stimulate but not to satisfy the interest in these documents, to set the reader on his way but not to carry him over the course. It makes no attempt at an exhaustive classification of the documents; still less does it endeavour to provide a complete commentary on any of them. But in the hope of drawing on readers to the study of the sources themselves it has been furnished with a fuller bibliography and more copious references than the scale of the work might seem to require.

Documents of later date than 146 B.C. have not been included in this survey, except in some special cases of more than ordinary interest.

I gratefully acknowledge the help and suggestions received from my former tutor, the Rev. E. M. Walker, and from Professor E. A. Gardner, Dr. G. Macdonald, and Mr. M. N. Tod. To Mr. Tod in particular I am much indebted for the generous way in which he has placed his profound knowledge of Greek inscriptions at my disposal.

M. CARY

CONTENTS

ABBREVIATIONS

Abb. Berl. Ak. = Abhandlungen der preussischen Akademie der Wissenschaften zu Berlin.

A.J.A. = American Journal of Archæology.

A.M. = Mitteilungen des deutschen archäologischen Instituts zu Athen.

A.S.A. = Annales du service des antiquités de l'Égypte.

B.C.H. = Bulletin de correspondance hellénique.

B.M. = The Collection of Ancient Greek Inscriptions in the British Museum.

B.S.A. = Annual of the British School at Athens.

Chrest. = Mitteis-Wilcken, Grundzüge und Chrestomathie der Papyruskunde.

C.Q. = Classical Quarterly.

D.S. = W. Dittenberger, Sylloge Inscriptionum Græcrum, 3rd edition.

'Εφ. 'Αρχ. = 'Εφημερὶς 'Αρχαιολογική.

F.D. = Th. Homolle, etc., Fouilles de Delphes.

H. = E. L. Hicks, Greek Historical Inscriptions.

H—H = E. L. Hicks and G. F. Hill, Greek Historical Inscriptions.

H.N.	= B. V. Head, Historia Numorum.
I.G.	= Inscriptiones Græcæ.
I.G. I.²	= Inscriptiones Græcæ, Editio Minor, Vol. I.
I.J.G.	= R. Dareste, B. Haussoullier, Th. Reinach, Recueil d'inscriptions juridiques grecques.
I.P.E.	= B. Latyschev and A. Pridik, Inscriptiones Antiquæ Oræ Septentrionalis Ponti Euxini Græcæ et Latinæ.
J.H.S.	= Journal of Hellenic Studies.
J.I.A.N.	= Journal international d'archéologie numismatique.
M.	= Ch. Michel, Recueil d'inscriptions grecques.
Magn.	= O. Kern, Die Inschriften von Magnesia-am-Mäander.
Milet	= Th. Wiegand, etc., Milet.
N.C.	= Numismatic Chronicle.
O.G.I.	= W. Dittenberger, Orientis Græci
	= Inscriptiones Selectæ.
Olymp.	= W. Dittenberger and K. Purgold, Die Inschriften von Olympia.
P. Eleph.	= O. Rubensohn, Die Elephantine Papyri.
Pergamon	= M. Fränkel, Die Inschriften von Pergamon.
P. Hibeh	= B. P. Grenfell and A. S. Hunt, The Hibeh Papyri.
P. Lond.	= F. G. Kenyon and H. I. Bell, Greek Papyri in the British Museum, London.

P. Ox.	= Grenfell and Hunt, The Oxyrhyn-chus Papyri.
P. Petr.	= J. P. Mahaffy and J. G. Smyly, The Petrie Papyri.
Priene	= Hiller von Gärtringen, Inschriften von Priene.
P.S.I.	= Papiri Greci e Latini della Societa Papirologica Italiana.
P. Tebt.	= Grenfell, Hunt, and Smyly, The Tebtunis Papyri, Vol. I.
P—Z	= H. v. Prott and L. Ziehen, Leges Græcorum Sacræ.
Rev. Phil.	= Revue de Philologie.
R—G	= E. S. Roberts and E. A. Gardner, Introduction to Greek Epigraphy.
Rhein. Mus.	= Rheinisches Museum für Philologie.
Riv. Fil.	= Rivista di Filologia.
S.-Ber. Berl.	= Sitzungsberichte der preussischen Akademie der Wissenschaften zu Berlin.
Schubart-Kühn	= W. Schubart and E. Kühn, Papyri und Ostraka der Ptolemäerzeit.
S.E.G.	= Supplementum Epigraphicum Græcum.

CHAPTER I

INTRODUCTORY

DOCUMENTARY evidence for Greek History first began to accumulate in the eighth century B.C. In the previous Dark Age the peoples of Greece had relapsed into illiteracy, and for the rough-and-ready methods of their tribal government and their self-contained economy they had little need of written records. But by the eighth century at the latest the alphabet was introduced into Greece, and in the city-states which were then being formed the technique of administration soon became elaborate enough to require written instruments.[1] First of all, lists of magistrates and priests were drawn up[2]; in the seventh century B.C. codes of law were compiled; in the sixth century treaties were drafted and resolutions of citizen assemblies were put on record. In the fifth century transactions of magistrates and of law courts were minuted; in the fourth and third centuries the public registration of private deeds came into use, and in some states was made com-

---

[1] This was especially the case in cities with a democratic constitution, where it was important to disseminate political knowledge among the general public.

[2] The list of victors at Olympia reached back to 776 B.C., that of Spartan ephors to 757 B.C., of Athenian archons to 683 B.C. The earliest entries in these lists may have been subsequently inserted from memory, but there no good reason for suspecting forgery, as in the case of the Roman fasti.

On the genuineness of the Olympian list, see especially A. Brinkmann in *Rhein. Mus.* 1915, p. 622 ff.

pulsory. Concurrently with these developments archive
houses were set up and secretariats were established.
In a fully fledged Greek state we may expect to find a
Public Record Office (ἀρχεῖον, βιβλιοφυλάκιον, etc.), a
Somerset House (συγγραφοφυλάκιον, χρεωφυλάκιον, etc.),
drafting clerks (γραμματεῖς, νομογράφοι), and custodians
of records (νομοφύλακες, χρεωφύλακες).[1]

The papyrus rolls (βύβλοι) on which the original
documents were ordinarily written[2] were stowed away
in chests (κιβώτια, γλωσσόκομα)[3] and were not acces-
sible to all comers. But copies (ἀντίγραφα) were frequently set up for public inspection. The greater
number of these was painted up on notice boards like
the "alba" of Italian towns, or on the walls of some
convenient public building or temple; but texts whose
contents were of more than passing interest were durab-
ly engraved on a wall or on a separate slab (στήλη) of
stone or, more rarely, of bronze, the cost of publication
often being borne by private individuals who had an
interest in the matter.[4] Treaties and transactions affecting more than one state were usually exhibited in several
places. Copies of the Peace of Nicias were set up on the
Acropolis of Athens, in the Spartan Amyclæum, at
Delphi and Olympia, and on the Isthmus of Corinth.[5]

[1] At Athens there was a general record office, the Μητρῷον. The drafting clerk was called γραμματεὺς τῆς βουλῆς, or κατὰ πρυτανείαν (Aristotle
᾿Αθηνάιων Πολιτέια, 54 §3). For other details, see M. Brillant, Les Secré-
taires athéniens.
[2] The use of parchment as an alternative material in the Hellenistic age is
attested in Priene No. 114 ls. 11, 30 (ἐν βυβλίνοις καὶ δερματικοῖς
τεύχεσιν).
[3] On Egyptian papyri we often find the archive-keeper's subscript
"Πέπτωκεν εἰς τὸ κιβώτιον."
[4] On the methods of publishing Greek records see especially Ad. Wilhelm,
Beiträge zur griechischen Inschriftenkunde, p. 229 ff., and Neue Beiträge, VI,
§47.   [5] Thuc. V, 18.

INTRODUCTORY 3

Similarly in a letter patent of Antiochus II of Syria it is directed that a certain transfer of land shall be advertised at Sardes, Ephesus, Didyma, Ilium, and Samothrace.[1]

While Greek governments thus were at pains to make their records known to their own public, Greek authors have only in rare cases reproduced them for the benefit of posterity. For our present knowledge of Greek documents we therefore depend mostly on the finds of travellers and excavators in modern times, thanks to whom we now possess many volumes of texts inscribed on papyrus, stone, clay, or bronze.[2]

Regarded as sources of historical knowledge, inscriptions and papyri have peculiar advantages and disadvantages. Their defects may be stated as follows:

(1) Inscriptions are capable of being forged, and by reason of their relative brevity they invite falsification.[3]

(2) The larger inscriptions, and papyri of all sizes, are usually found in a more or less mutilated condition. In many cases the texts defy restoration; in others, and these are the most dangerous, they are just complete enough to tempt us into plausible but uncertain emendations. Before drawing conclusions from the restored texts of inscriptions or papyri, historians must observe

[1] *O.G.I.* 225.

[2] Travellers have scoured the Levant for inscriptions since the days of Cyriacus of Ancona (c. 1435 A.D.). The excavations on which we now chiefly depend for epigraphic finds have been proceeding steadily during the last fifty years. The systematic search for papyri began some thirty years ago, when Petrie first detached them from mummy-wrappings, and Grenfell and Hunt excavated them in the rubbish-heaps of the Fayum.

[3] Many texts were forged in the sixteenth century by the notorious Pirro Ligorio, and in the eighteenth century by the Abbé Fourmont. For possible recent instances, cf. J. Svoronos in *J.I.A.N.*, 1920, p. 12 ff., where the text *B.M.* 935 (=*I.G.* I² 975) is declared a forgery, and the alleged Cypselid inscription on a gold cup of the Boston Museum. (*J.H.S.* 1925, p. 114 and n. 146.)

4 SOURCES OF GREEK HISTORY

whether the words on which they base their inferences are actually legible in the document or have been inserted by the modern editor, and in the latter case they must consider whether the editor's restorations are anything better than mere guesswork.

Of the numerous instances in which this precaution has been disregarded the following is worth special mention. In 1902 a new papyrus was published, which at first was given out as a history of Athens by a well-informed antiquarian of the Hellenistic period, containing important new facts about the building of the Parthenon, the transfer of federal funds from Delos to Athens, and constitutional changes following the deposition of the Thirty Tyrants.[1] These alleged new facts were making their way into history books, when it was discovered that many emendations in the original edition were faulty, that the papyrus really was a table of contents prefixed to a biography of Demosthenes, and that it contained no new information of any consequence.[2]

(3) The dating of inscriptions is often attended with difficulties. The custom of affixing dates to documents was not introduced into Greece until the fifth century. From about 450 B.C. public acts at Athens usually carried the name of the archon eponymus and of the prytany under which they were issued,[3] and in the fourth century the use of similar date marks became general among Greek states. But the reckoning over of a Greek magistrate-year or priest-year into the corres-

[1] B. Keil, *Anonymus Argentinensis.*
[2] U. Wilcken, *Hermes* 1907, p. 374 ff., and R. Laqueur, *ibid.* 1908, p. 219ff.
[3] The earliest dated inscription is a decree of 485-4 B.C., relating to religious ritual (R—G 132; *I.G.* I.², 3-4). The earliest political document with an archon date belongs to 454-3 B.C. (*I.G.* I.² 191.)

ponding year B.C. cannot be reduced to a simple rule, except in some rare cases where we possess a continuous list of eponymi in their correct order. Unfortunately Greek officials did not follow the example of Greek historians from the third century onward in dating by Olympiads, under which system it is possible to synchronise with the Christian era by a simple reckoning.[1] The inscriptions of the Hellenistic monarchies also offer chronological problems, for while these regularly give the name of the reigning sovereign they do not always mention the year of the reign.

Lastly, minor perplexities arise from the lack of a set rule for equating Attic prytanies with the months of the calendar year, and of synchronising the lunar years of the various Greek states with our solar years.

In the absence of a date mark, it is true, we may find a clue in the letter forms, the orthography or grammar of inscriptions, but in applying these rough tests we must allow for a margin of error of at least twenty-five years.[2]

In general, the inscriptions of 450–300 B.C. can be dated accurately; the earlier ones, and many documents of the third century,[3] can only be provided with approximate dates.

The dating of official papyri is relatively easy, for these usually give the year of the reigning sovereign

[1] An exceptional case is the mention of an Olympian and a Pythian victor in an inscription of 220 B.C. from Magnesia. (*Magn.* 16.)

[2] For a survey of letter forms, see E. S. Roberts and E. A. Gardner, *Introduction to Greek Epigraphy*, Vol. I. For the orthographic and grammatical usages, see K. Meisterhans, *Grammatik der griechischen Inschriften* (3rd ed., by E. Schwyzer, 1900).

[3] For a summary of recent discussions on the chronology of third century documents, see Tod, *J.H.S.* 1925, pp. 109-110, 116.

and often provide the names of one or more eponymous priests into the bargain.[1]

(4) Of the surviving inscriptions less than half belong to the period before Alexander, and only a small fraction are anterior to 400 B.C. Of the extant papyri the great majority are of the Roman or Byzantine era, and very few are of earlier date than 275 B.C.[2] Moreover, since these documents are mostly derived from up-country towns, they seldom throw any light on high politics.

(5) Inscriptions and papyri provide the skeleton, but they do not supply the flesh and blood, of history. For a full appreciation of men's actions and motives we cannot dispense with literary sources, and where these fail us, as in some periods of the Hellenistic era, we cannot hope to restore our historical personages to full life.

But on closer inspection the faults of inscriptions and papyri are less serious than they appear at first sight, and they are set off by some peculiar and substantial merits.

(1) The precautions now taken by the discoverers and editors of epigraphic texts have reduced the risk of successful counterfeiting to a minimum. During the last fifty years it has become the regular practice to provide the means of testing every new find by giving an exact description of its locality and supplying, wherever possible, a photographic copy or a squeeze. Besides, the study of Greek letter forms and of the phraseology of each class of document has been carried to such a point

---

[1] The papyri of the third century are dated by Macedonian lunar months, which are an occasional source of trouble. (See the discussion in *Hibeh Papyri*, p. 332 ff.)

[2] The two chief collections in Britain, the British Museum and the Oxyrhynchus papyri, are mostly of the second and subsequent centuries A.D.

that no epigraphic expert is likely to be deceived by a forgery, save perhaps at the hands of another expert.

(2) The restoration of texts on stone and papyrus has ceased to be a mere gamble and is being reduced to a science like the emendation of literary MSS. On the public inscriptions of the fifth and fourth centuries the work of supplying missing letters is greatly facilitated by the fact that the stone-cutters of this period executed their work στοιχηδόν, i.e., they spaced out their texts so as to provide an equal number of letters to each line. Furthermore, in official documents of every period certain set phrases and common-form expressions recur with monotonous regularity. Therefore, when once we have learnt the standard formulæ in any one type of act, such as a treaty or a complimentary decree, we may apply them confidently to the restoration of other texts of the same class. As an object lesson in the scientific character of text restoration as now practised by the best scholars, attention may be drawn to the work of the Austrian epigraphist, Ad. Wilhelm,[1] the study of which will instruct more than a whole handbook of directions.

(3) Though none of our eponymous lists is quite complete, the gaps in them are being steadily reduced, and new catalogues are being from time to time discovered. Fifty years ago our only continuous list was that of the Attic archons from 481-0 to 293-2 B.C., which could be compiled from the annalistic entries of Diodorus and Dionysius of Halicarnassus. This list has since been prolonged in an almost unbroken series to 31 B.C.[2]

[1] In the *Beiträge* and *Neue Beiträge* quoted on p. 3, and in the *Wiener Anzeiger*.

[2] For a recent discovery of two new names, see Tod, *loc. cit.* pp. 109-110.

8 SOURCES OF GREEK HISTORY

From Delos we now possess a table of archons extending from 302 to 166 B.C., in which only four names are missing,[1] and from Miletus we have a series of eponymi which extends unbroken from 523 to 260 B.C., and thence with occasional gaps to 32 A.D.[2]

The arrangement of the Attic archon list has also been greatly facilitated by the discovery of "Ferguson's Law," which declares that from 363-2 B.C. the Attic tribes took it in turns to provide the Secretary of Council for the current year.[3] Thus whenever an archon can be synchronised with a secretary, his place within the "cycle of secretaries" is fixed, and if there is further evidence to show to which particular secretary-cycle he belonged, his date B.C. can be determined. The cycle was occasionally interrupted, but Ferguson's law holds good for most of the period 357–104 B.C.

With the help of these and similar new data, the margin of error in the chronology of our inscribed texts is growing less and less.

(4) The comparative lateness of our inscriptions and papyri is not altogether to be regretted, for they become numerous just at the point where our literary texts grow scanty. It is not too much to say that the writing of an adequate history of Hellenistic Greece has only become possible since the newly discovered documentary texts of that period have begun to accumulate. Moreover, it is no great disadvantage that Ptolemaic papyri deal mostly with minor officials and folk in humble walks of life, for it is about these that we most require fresh knowledge.

[1] See the Introduction to *I.G.* XI. 2 pp. vi-vii.
[2] See Ch. V. p. 59.
[3] W. S. Ferguson, *Cornell Studies in Classical Philology*, Vol. VII.

(5) If Greek inscriptions and papyri do not reveal the whole truth, in general they reveal nothing but the truth. They are as a rule composed *sine studio et ira*, and with a particular regard to accuracy of expression. Furthermore, in regard to the quantity and variety of information which they provide, they form not merely a casual adjunct but an indispensable companion to our literary sources.[1]

In the following chapters the various classes of documents, whether derived from books, inscriptions or papyri, will be passed under review.

[1] Writing some forty years ago, Dr. Jowett (*Thucydides*. Introduction to second edition) was perhaps justified in belittling the quantitative contribution of non-literary sources to our knowledge of Greek history. At the present time such disparagement would be a mark of sheer ignorance.

CHAPTER II

LAWS

IN this chapter we shall consider the remains of Greek law codes and specimens of individual laws. In Chapter III we shall survey other regulative acts of Greek legislatures which may be comprised under the name of "decrees." The difference between these two classes of measures is that the laws were intended to be permanent, whereas the decrees prescribed for particular cases. This classification ignores the technical distinction drawn at Athens and elsewhere between νόμοι and ψηφίσματα, which differed only in that ψηφίσματα which had been confirmed by a special revisory board of νομοθέται or νομογράφοι were promoted to the status of νόμοι. This distinction was quite arbitrary, and a good many acts which in strict legal parlance remained ψηφίσματα nevertheless had the effect of laws.

I. CODES. (a) Athens. The codes of Draco and Solon were originally inscribed on wooden boards set edge to edge round a revolving pillar (ἄξονες). Stone copies of Solon's laws, similarly mounted (κύρβεις), were also set up for public inspection[1]; and in 409 B.C. a transcription of Draco's code, or of such parts as then survived, on stone slabs was ordered.

Of these texts nothing now remains save one slab

[1] On the ἄξονες and κύρβεις see especially Busolt, *Griechische Geschichte* II, p. 291 n. 3.

from the reproduction of Draco's code.¹ Fortunately
several statutes from either code have been quoted more
or less fully by the Attic orators and other writers. It
is true that some of the documents which appear in the
texts of the orators, notably those in Demosthenes' *In
Midiam* and *De Corona*, and Æschines' *In Timarchum*,
have been proved to be later interpolations of no historical value. But the great majority have been shown
to be genuine and to contain at any rate the substance
of the laws quoted.²

The surviving fragments of Draco's code are sufficient to establish the important fact that the Attic law
of his day already observed the distinction between
killing and murder. Vendettas were severely restricted,
and a board of referees (ἐφέται) was provided to define
the degree of guilt in each case.³

The remaining specimens of Solon's legislation are
mostly short excerpts in the Attic orators. The most
important of the fragments prescribes revised regulations for the trial of homicide: not only ephetæ and
Areopagus, but archons and Heliæa play a part.⁴
Solon's Heliæa also figures in a punitive statute which
authorised it to supplement the ordinary money penalties for theft by lodging the delinquent in the stocks.⁵
Of Solon's sundry regulations in matters of civil law his
most notable is a statute conceding freedom of testa-

¹ H—H 78; better texts in DS 111; *I.G.* I² 115.
² See especially E. Drerup, *Jahrbücher für klassische Philologie, Supplement*
24, p. 221-366. Drerup chiefly bases his proof on the names and dates given
in the documents, and on their formulation.
³ Besides H—H 78 see [Demosthenes] 43, §57.
⁴ Demosthenes 23 §§ 22-60. A clause quoted in §51 is ascribed by Demosthenes to Draco. Presumably it was a Draconian measure which Solon
took over.
⁵ Lysias 10 § 16; Dem. 24 § 105.

SOURCES OF GREEK HISTORY

ment to persons having no male issue and not acting under the influence of drugs.[1] Others of his measures prohibited vain display at funerals[2] and placed restrictions upon builders and planters in the interests of adjacent properties.[3] Of Solon's constitutional laws nothing survives in the actual text.

Of Cleisthenes' legislation nothing is preserved unless it be a curt sentence to the effect that "the phratores must perforce admit both the worshippers and the milk-brothers,"[4] whatever that may mean. His constitutional laws were not quoted by the Attic orators, for such of them as had not been superseded by the fourth century had become too familiar to require reiteration. Moreover it is probable that his code was never copied on stone, for in 411 B.C. a legislative commission which required a text of his statutes had to be directed to "make a search for them" (προσαναζητῆσαι), presumably in the recesses of he archives.[5]

Of Pericles' measures not a single text remains, and of the legislation of the Peloponnesian War we only possess the "psephism of Diophantus" (410 B.C.), by which all assailants of the restored democracy were outlawed *ipso facto*.[6]

The revised code of 403 B.C. survives in many small samples inside the texts of the Attic orators. One of these is the psephism of Tisamenus, which reinstated

[1] [Dem.] 46 § 14.
[2] [Dem.] 43 § 62. For similar laws at Julis in Ceos and Gambreum in Mysia see DS 1218-9 or *I.J.G.* I. 2 and 3.
[3] *Digest* X 1, 13. The Digest also quotes from Solon a law conceding the right of association for worship, trade or piracy (XLVII. 22. 4). But the mention of δῆμοι in this text suggests that it is not anterior to Cleisthenes.
[4] Quoted by Philochorus, fr. 94.
[5] Ἀθ. Πολ. 29 § 3.
[6] Andocides I § 96.

the codes of Draco and Solon after their suspension by the Thirty Tyrants and instructed the Areopagus to mount guard over them.[1] Another is a redraft of the old regulation which declared invalid all statutes concerning individuals (νόμοι ἐπ᾽ ἀνδρί) unless enacted by secret ballot on a poll of not less than 6,000.[2] Further regulations provided for the periodic revision of the laws by a special jury of Nomothetæ,[3] debarred the Ecclesia from abrogating or overriding measures thus confirmed,[4] and forbade magistrates and courts of justice to apply unwritten law.[5] To these statutes may be added the revised oath of the Heliasts, by which jurors bound themselves to countenance no revolution, political or social.[6]

(b) *Gortyn.* The nearest approach to a complete statute book has come down to us in an inscription of 640 lines from Gortyn in Crete.[7] The technical terminology and the Doric dialect of this text create many difficulties of interpretation, and its date is so uncertain that some scholars assign it to the sixth century, while others, probably with better reason, attribute parts to the fifth century and the rest to the fourth. Yet the Law of Gortyn is of unique value, because it shows more

[1] Andoc. I. §§ 83-4. *cf.* Dem. 24 § 42.
[2] Andoc. I, § 87; Dem. 23 § 86, 24 § 59.
[3] Dem. 24 §§ 20-23. On the genuineness of this text, see R. Schöll, *Sitzungsberichte Bairische Akademie*, philologisch-philosophische Klasse 1886, p. 83-139.
[4] Andoc. I, § 87; Dem. 23 § 87; 24 § 33.
[5] Andoc. I, § 85.
[6] Dem. 24 §§ 149-151.
[7] The text, with translation and full commentary, is given in *I.J.G.* I, 17-18. See also J. Kohler and E. Ziebarth, *Das Stadtrecht von Gortyn*, and the analysis by W. Wyse and F. E. Adcock in the *Cambridge Companion to Greek Studies* (3rd ed.), p. 465 ff. On a short fragment of a code from Eltynia, prescribing compensations for assault (with or without a bloody nose), *cf. S.E.G.* III, 509.

clearly than any other Greek document, or the Twelve
Tables of Rome, the transition from the rough justice
of a patriarchal society to the humaner code of a city-
state. Harsh usages and unscientific procedure are indeed still to be found in it. Enslavement for debt is
recognised and penalties vary according to the status
of the injured party, judges are bound by sworn declara-
tions of witnesses, and written evidence is not yet
admitted. On the other hand the Law admits the right
of sons to hold property in their own name and secures
a share of inheritances for daughters; above all, it pro-
tects slaves against their masters. The equitableness of
the Gortyn code belies the general bad reputation of the
Cretans.

(c) *Alexandria.* The next longest collection of laws
stands on a papyrus containing an extract from the
municipal code of Alexandria.[1] The measures here
transcribed include a set of building regulations, a
clause exempting royal officials from arrest, and a dis-
pensation from payment of the salt *octroi* in favour of
teachers. The first of these laws copies closely the statute of Solon (p. 12)[2]; the last is a modest anticipation
of the indulgences bestowed upon teachers by the
Cæsars.

It is mentioned by Strabo, as if it were something
uncommon, that the statutes of Massilia were on public
view.[3] This suggests that Greek codes were not usually
exhibited in durable stone copies. Whether this be the

---

[1] Text and commentary in *Dikaiomata*, by F. Bechtel and others (Berlin,
1913).
[2] In another fragment of an Egyptian municipal code, relating to com-
plaints by freemen against slaves, Athenian procedure is copied, but with
variations of detail (*P. Lille* I, 29).
[3] IV, 1, 5 (p. 179).

reason or no, the surviving remains are disappointingly few.

II. SINGLE STATUTES. (*a*) *Constitutional.*

Athenian dependencies. Of the constitutions imposed by Athens upon her colonists and allies in the Confederacy of Delos we have only a few fragments which compare poorly with some of the well-preserved *leges datæ* of Roman colonies or municipia. The most important remnant is an inscription of *c.* 460 B.C., in which the government of Erythræ is recast on an obviously Athenian pattern.[1]

The Hellenic Leagues of Philip and Demetrius. Two important inscriptions throw light on the constitutional aspect of Macedonian rule in Greece. One· of these preserves the oath of loyalty to Philip sworn by the Greek confederates at Corinth in 337 B.C., and part of a list of cities and territories, against each of which stands a figure indicating the number of its deputies in the Hellenic parliament.[2] The other document sets forth the terms of the covenant imposed by Demetrius in 302 B.C.[3] These conditions are closely modelled on those of Philip's constitution, but they contain some novel clauses about the functions and powers of a Greek federal parliament.

Chios. On a stone κύρβις from this island is inscribed a fragment of a constitution similar in character and date to that of Solon.[4] The mention of δήμου ῥῆτραι and of δήμαρχοι in this text suggests a compact be-

[1] H—H 32. A more recent text in DS 41; S.E.G. I. 2.
[2] DS 260; Ad. Wilhelm, *Attische Urkunden* I.
[3] *S.E.G.* I. 75; Ad. Wilhelm, *Wiener Anzeiger* 1922, p. 52-70; W. Tarn, *J.H.S.* 1922, p. 198 ff.
[4] Text and commentary by U. v. Wilamowitz-Moellendorff, *Abh. Berl. Ak.* 1908, p. 64 ff; by E. Nachmanson in *Historische griechische Inschriften* No. 2.

tween people's deputies and kings or nobles, like those
which the ephors struck at Sparta and the tribunes at
Rome; the reference to a βουλὴ δημοσίη which could
hear appeals and impose fines invites comparison with
Solon's Four Hundred.

Miscellaneous. A considerable number of extant
Greek statutes betrays the same anxiety to avert revolution as is evident in the Athenian legislation of 403 B.C.
(pp. 12-3). A large proportion of these measures belongs
to the wild age of the Diadochi, when the governments
of the cities were menaced alike by democrats, oligarchs,
and tyrants. In several states the entire citizen body was
sworn in against treason,[1] and at Ilium tyrants and oligarchs, and all their aiders and abettors, were threat-
ened with economic boycott, assassination, and *dam-
natio memoriæ*.[2] From Teos we have a law of *c.* 470 B.C.
containing a collective imprecation upon treason, piracy, black magic, and attacks upon the people's food.[3]
The lighter side is illustrated by a third-century law of
Iasus which lays down meticulous rules for the distribution of ecclesiasts' pay and takes elaborate precautions against fraudulent claims.[4]

(*b*) *Financial statutes.* The principal financial law
from Athens is the "Decree of Callias," which made
provision for better administration of the temple funds
and safeguarded the deposits against hasty borrowing.[5]
Though this document is assigned by some authorities
to 420–17 B.C., it more probably belongs to 435–3 B.C.,
and may in that case be regarded as a battening of

---

[1] M 1316 (Chersonesus in Crimea); M 1317 (Itanus in Crete).
[2] M 524.
[3] H—H 23; DS 37-8.
[4] M 466.
[5] H—H 49; DS 91.

the hatches before the storm of the Peloponnesian War.[1]

A common form of statute in the Hellenistic age was the deed of trust by which the administration of municipal endowments was regulated. From Delphi we have two laws of the second century by which a corn-purchase fund, a school fund, and a holiday fund were established out of sums supplied by the kings of Pergamum.[2] From Samos we possess a long text of similar date in which a capital raised by public inscription is made over to a committee with instructions to buy corn at harvest time and to practise usury at other seasons.[3] From Teos and Miletus two valuable inscriptions of 250–200 B.C. survive, relating to the endowment of secondary schools.[4] These documents throw much light on the staffing of secondary schools, the teachers' rates of pay, the admission of girl pupils (as at Teos), and the duties of education ministers.

Greek laws in restraint of trade appear to have been less numerous than Greek economic literature would suggest. Of the various regulations by which the Athenians sought to secure their food supply only one is known to us *verbatim*, viz., a law forbidding loans to shippers save on condition that their return cargo should consist of corn.[5] Other experiments in state control are exemplified by an attempt of the Delphians to reduce interest to the low rate of 6 per cent. (*c.* 400 B.C.)[6]; by a Delian law regulating the sale of charcoal to the detri-

[1] On this point see especially G. H. Stevenson in *J.H.S.* 1924, p. 1 ff.
[2] DS 671-2 (162-0 B.C.).
[3] DS 976. Commentary by U. v. Wilamowitz-Moellendorff and Th. Wiegand in *S-Ber. Berl.* 1904, p. 917 ff.
[4] DS 577-8. Commentaries in E. Ziebarth, *Aus dem griechischen Schulwesen*, and B. Laum, *Stiftungen in der griechischen und römischen Antike.*
[5] [Dem.] 35 § 51.   [6] *F.D.* III, 1, 94.

ment of engrossers (c. 250 B.C.);[1] and by a text of Olbia
compelling foreign merchants to exchange their coin
for Olbian currency "at the stone in the Place of
Assembly."[2] The general simplicity of Greek customs
regulations is illustrated by a tariff from Cyparissia in
Messenia, prescribing a flat rate of 2 per cent.[3]

The comparative paucity of financial records is com-
pensated by the fullness of one remaining specimen, the
"Revenue Law of Ptolemy Philadelphus."[4] This document, the longest of our non-literary papyri, consists of
a series of royal ordinances of a fiscal character. It
contains minute prescriptions of rights and duties for
the contractors who collected the quotas on orchard
produce, provisions for the secularising of temple dues
on the sale of wine, and a complete code regulating the
production and sale of various oils. It compelled the
tax-farmers to show monthly accounts to the government auditor and carefully safeguarded the interests of
the Crown; yet it left the cultivators exposed to seizures
by the tax-collectors and coercion by armed troops.
Part of these measures is reproduced in the *Lex Hiero-
nica* of Syracuse and the Roman *leges publicorum vendun-
dorum*.[5] The paragraphs relating to the production and
sale of oil are a good instance of government control run
mad. The growers, including several great temple
corporations, are required to plant on prescribed lines
and sell to middlemen who in turn must retail at specified prices. Imports of foreign oil are prohibited, except

[1] DS 975.
[2] DS 218.
[3] DS 952. For a more complex tariff at Palmyra under the Roman
Empire, see *O.G.I.* 629.
[4] Text and commentary by B. P. Grenfell and J. P. Mahaffy.
[5] On this point see M. Rostovtseff, *Geschichte des römischen Kolonats* Ch.III,
and J Carcopino, *La Loi de Hiéron*, p. 65 ff.

small quantities of olive oil which are admitted under a tariff, and the police are charged to detect the inevitable leakages in this monopoly.

(c) *Laws relating to religion.* The right of the state to control religion was generally admitted and unsparingly exercised in Greece. Numerous inscriptions illustrate this Erastian attitude.

The series of Athenian acts begins with a measure 485-84 B.C., containing rules for the attendants at the archaic sanctuary of Athena[1] : they must open the shrine to the public at least twice a month, must remove nothing from the precincts, must neither build nor set up ovens on the Acropolis. By a statute of *c.* 460 B.C. the ritual at the Eleusinian mysteries was regulated and a truce imposed upon participant states.[2] In 423-2 B.C. a second law provided for the collection and storage of Eleusinian tithes and the delimitation of the Pelargicum under the Acropolis.[3] In 335-4 B.C. the ritual at the Panathenaea was regulated afresh in a measure which betrays the antiquarian zeal of the orator Lycurgus.[4]

An Amphictyonic law of historical interest survives in an inscription from Delphi (*c.* 380 B.C.) which orders a periodical beating of the bounds round Apollo's sanctuary and prescribes penalties for transgressors.[5] It was presumably under this act that the Phocians were prosecuted in 356 B.C. A Tegean law of similar date deals with sacred lands in a more generous spirit, for it allows priests to pasture twenty-five head of sheep on it

[1] R—G 132; *I.G.* I² 3-4.
[2] *B.M.* 2; DS 42.
[3] *R—G* 9; DS 83. I here follow the date given in Dittenberger's edition.
[4] DS 271.
[5] *R—G* 70; DS 145.

and visitors to graze their draught cattle for twenty-four hours.[1]

A highly detailed regulation from Andania (in Messenia) relating to the local mysteries of Demeter gives a good idea of a Greek πανήγυρις with its large concourse of visitors and attendant fair.[2] *Inter alia*, this act prescribes the costumes to be worn, the space allotted to camping parties, and the rules for buyers and sellers at the market.

The laws relating to the appointment of priesthoods usually prescribed physical soundness,[3] the attainment of a certain age (in some cases not more than ten years),[4] and the punctual payment of each instalment of purchase money[5]; they are remarkably reticent as to good conduct or religious learning.   The payment of priests usually took the form of perquisites from the sacrifices, e.g., the loins, kidneys, rumps, hams, and tongues (but not the hides) of the victims[6].   At Priene the priest of Dionysus was progressively exempted from the lighter and the heavier liturgies (or public services) as the price of purchase rose[7]; at Miletus the priest "of the people of Rome and of Rome" received a money stipend of 600 drachms,[8] and at Halicarnassus a priestess was authorised to make street collections.[9]

(*d*) *Bye-laws*. Except in matters pertaining to reli-

[1] M 695.
[2] DS 736.
[3] DS 1012, l. 9.
[4] DS 1012, l. 10.
[5] M 732.
[6] DS 1002 (Miletus).   *Cf.* DS 1013 (Chios).
[7] *Priene* 174.   *Cf.* also *Priene* 201 (privileges of the priest of Poseidon Heliconius).
[8] *Milet*, Vol. I, Pt. 7, no. 203.   This priesthood was founded during the ascendancy of the Gracchi at Rome.
[9] *B.M.* 895; DS 1015.

gion, the legislative powers of subordinate authorities
in Greek states were severely restricted. Legislation by
an Attic deme is exemplified by an act of the Myr-
rhinusians, relating to the audit of the local accounts
(fourth century).[1] The procedure laid down for the
δήμαρχος, the λογισταί and εὔθυναι is closely modelled
on that of the corresponding officials at Athens. The
activities of an Attic phratry may be studied in a long
inscription containing a series of regulations for admission among the Demotionidae (early fourth century).[2] An ironical commentary on these rules is
provided by a contemporaneous phratry list which
contains no more than twenty names.[3]

The subdivisions of a Greek city in Egypt, probably
Alexandria itself, are the subject of a papyrus text
which unfortunately is very incomplete. So much can
be made out, that the town was divided into 5 φυλαί,
60 δῆμοι, and 720 φρατρίαι.[4]

The ordinances set up by temple authorities are
extremely numerous. Most of them relate to ceremonial
procedure, or to the terms of admission to the precincts.
Among the texts which deal with ritual we may mention
an inscription from Miletus which regulates the pro-
cession to the temple at Didyma and the pæans sung
on the way by a gild of μολποί (fifth century)[5]; a puri-
tanical notice at a Thasian sanctuary—"no sheep, no
pigs, no pæans here"[6]—; a list of sacrificial rules at
Cos, prescribing distinctive offerings from various cal-

---

[1] M 150.
[2] R—G 84; DS 921; I.J.G. II, 29 (with commentary).
[3] I.J.G. II, 29a; M 1545.
[4] P. Hibeh 28; Chrest., 25.
[5] DS 57.
[6] M 706.

lings and estates[1], the order of procedure at an athletic festival at Ceos[2]; sacrificial calendars from Athens[3] and Myconos.[4]

Among the rules laid down for worshippers the most notable are the dormitory regulations at the incubation oracle of Amphiaraus at Oropus,[5] and a miscellany of taboos on unclean objects. The articles banned include gay clothes,[6] shoe-leather,[7] cheese,[8] Dorians,[9] and women.[10]

[1] M 720. [2] M 402.
[3] R—G 138, 142. [4] M 714. [5] M 698.
[6] P—Z. II, 90-91 (Delos). [7] M 434 (Ialysus). [8] M 723 (Lindus).
[9] P—Z. II, 106 (Paros).
[10] P—Z. II, 79 (Elatea); II, 105 (Paros); S.E.G. II, 505 (Thasos). On the Subject of taboos, see T. Wächter, *Reinheitsvorschriften im griechischen Kult.*

CHAPTER III

DECREES RELATING TO HOME AFFAIRS

ENACTMENTS of Greek cities relating to some particular situation or affecting some particular set of persons have survived in relatively large numbers, the reason for this being that it was often in the interest of one or other of the parties concerned to provide a durable copy of the decree. Some typical specimens of this class of documents will be reviewed in this and the next chapter.

(1) Acts Relating to Internal Affairs.

(a) *Party Politics.* The vehemence with which party strife was pursued in Greek cities is reflected in a characteristic group of records. Some of these reveal the lighter aspects of στάσις. Thus in an inscription from Erythræ (c. 332 B.C.) we read a resolution that a new sword should be fitted to the statue of a tyrannicide whom a previous oligarchy had despoiled.[1] But the majority of the documents deal with the difficult problem of finding terms of settlement between contending parties. From Athens we have Solon's act of recall in favour of political outlaws,[2] and a decree passed after the disaster of Aegospotami which is an expansion of Solon's measure.[3] From Thasos we possess a pro-

---

[1] H—H 159; DS 284.
[2] Plutarch, *Solon*, Ch. 19.
[3] Andoc. I, §§ 77-9.

clamation inviting exiles home after the oligarchic revolution of 411 B.C.[1] But the real crux of a compromise after στάσις lay in the liquidation of claims by restored outlaws to their former property. The documents show that solutions to this problem differed widely. In an early text from Halicarnassus (c. 460 B.C.) all claims, if properly certified and registered by a given date, are allowed without further hearing, and no compensation is offered to the dispossessed.[2] In the inscriptions of Alexander's time more equitable expedients are prescribed. At Mytilene a mixed commission was set up to sift claims, the Council was empowered to resolve deadlocks, and the magistrates were charged to prevent acts of retaliation.[3] At Tegea the Ecclesia confirmed a set of rules drawn up in Alexander's own chancery: houses and gardens were to be retained, marriage-knots between Montagues and Capulets to remain tied, outstanding disputes to go to a neutral court at Mantinea.[4] At Ephesus a financial crisis precipitated by στάσις (297 B.C.) was averted by a compromise which recalls the famous debt-settlement of Lucullus in 70 B.C.[5] In an Athenian inscription of 352 B.C., we read of a dispute concerning a trespass upon the temple land at Eleusis. By a curious procedure this was referred for solution to Delphi, although Delphi itself was at that time in the hands of trespassers.[6] Instances of judicial proceedings against defeated revolutionaries among the

[1] *A.M.* 1903 p. 437 ff.
[2] H—H 27; D 45.
[3] H—H 164; M 356.
[4] DS 306. In a letter to Chios Alexander curtly ordered the restoration of exiles, irrespective of ways and means (H—H 158; DS 283).
[5] DS 364. For a similar enactment at Ephesus during the First Mithridatic War, see H 205; *I.J.G.* I. 4 (with commentary).
[6] R—G 36; DS 204.

subject-allies of Athens will be considered in Ch. IV (pp. 42-3). A pathetic confession of failure to deal with στάσις is recorded in a fifth century inscription from Dodona: "the Corcyræans communicate a suit to Zeus Naus and Diona, to which god or hero should they sacrifice and pray to obtain the blessing of concord?"[1]

(*b*) *Finance: Assessment orders.* One invaluable document relating to the Delian Confederacy, the decree for re-assessment of the subject-allies in 425 B.C., has been preserved. On this inscription we may study point for point the careful and scrupulous procedure prescribed by the Athenian Ecclesia.[2]

Leases. The methods of leasing public lands are copiously illustrated by inscriptions. A fifth-century contract from Ceos retains a primitive simplicity: the tenant shall pay 30 drachmas on the tenth of Bacchion; if he does not pay, he shall quit; he shall keep the house standing and roofed; he shall not cut down fruit trees.[3] Later on the terms become more explicit, sometimes the estates are described and delimited with the meticulousness of a modern conveyance deed.[4] A notable feature of these leases is the emphasis laid on good cultivation in the vine and olive yards, and the comparative neglect of the tillage land.[5] The leases on Egyptian papyri are mostly private documents (see Ch. VIII, p. 91), but in one compact we read of a reservist soldier renting a small oil plantation from the

---

[1] M 843. [2] H—H 64; *I.G.* I² 63.
[3] M 1352. *Cf.* also the lease of the τέμενος of Codrus at Athens in 418/7 B.C. (DS 93). This is couched in terms hardly less simple.
[4] See especially a decree of an Attic phratry in M 1357 and a long text from Heraclea in S. Italy (*I.J.G.* I, 12, with commentary).
[5] *E.g.* in the text from Heraclea (n. 4 above), and in leases of the Attic deme of Aixoneis (R—G 129; DS 966) and of Arcesine on Amorgos (DS 963). See also R—G 131; *I.J.G.* I, 13 (miscellaneous contracts).

Crown and agreeing to sell the entire produce to the government.[1] This document aptly illustrates the Revenue Law discussed in Ch. II (pp. 18-9). The rules for letting public buildings may be studied in a decree of the deme of Piracus. The town theatre is knocked down to the highest bidder, and the lessee is required to find wooden benches for the spectators (fourth century).[2]

Public loans. Resolutions inviting loans are not so common as the tendency of Greek cities to reckless borrowing might suggest. But some interesting specimens have survived. At Oropus the war minister is instructed to collect funds wherever obtainable; lenders of one talent are to receive προξενία; for lesser contributors suitable consolation prizes are offered (late third century).[3] At Arcesine a Naxian who had lent three talents at the moderate rate of 10 per cent. is empowered to distrain without warrant upon any citizen or metic property (c. 300 B.C.).[4]

Public works. Decrees relating to the construction or repair of public buildings are specially common in Attica. From the Periclean age we have a measure providing for the erection of the temple of Athena Nike according to the specifications of Callicrates,[5] and another ordering a repair of a gap in the Acropolis wall, through which the stones for the Parthenon had presumably been hauled.[6] The solicitude for economy which we noted in the "Callias decree" (Ch. II, p. 22) is also expressed in a resolution of similar date which invites opinions from citizens and even from subject allies, whether certain repairs on the Hecatompedus

---

[1] *P. Hamburg* I, 24 (222 B.C.).   [2] M 143.   [3] M 587.
[4] DS 955; *I.J.G.* I, 15.   [5] H—H 37.   [6] *I.G.* I² 44.

temple should be executed in gold and ivory or in copper.[1] In a long text of 346 B.C. we read the specifications of Philo for the naval arsenal at Zea: walls of Piræus limestone, architraves of Hymettus or Pentelicus marble, roofing tiles from Corinth, a hundred other minutiae of measurement and materials.[2] In a decree of 337 B.C., which was plainly inspired by Demosthenes, detailed instructions are given for the repair of the Piræus walls.[3] To the same period belongs an order made on the motion of Demades for levelling the market square in Piræus and for keeping it in future free of rubbish heaps and encumbrances.[4]

Of ædilician documents from other parts of Greece we may mention a text of 189 lines with specifications for a temple at Lebadea (second century),[5] and an even longer set of instructions to the police of Pergamum regarding the maintenance of streets, wells, and buildings.[6]

(2) ACTS RELATING TO INDIVIDUALS. (ψηφίσματα ἐπ' ἀνδρί.)

Sentences of punishment passed by Greek Ecclesiæ in their judicial capacity will be treated along with other judicial records in Ch. VI. The decrees here quoted are records of benefits conferred. Such records were often set up on durable slabs at the beneficiary's cost; hence the ratio of surviving specimens of this class is unusually high.[7]

Enfranchisements.—The exclusiveness of Greek cities

---

[1] *S.E.G.* I, 3, and II, 2. For the date (433/2 B.C.), see A. J. Dinsmoor in *A.J.A.* 1923, p. 318.
[2] R—G 126; DS 969.   [3] M 1465.   [4] R—G 47; DS 313.
[5] DS 972.   [6] *O.G.I.* 483.
[7] On the whole subject of public honours, see Larfeld, *Griechische Epigraphik*, p. 381 ff.

in the fifth and fourth centuries is reflected in the
paucity of enfranchisement acts of that period. The
principal documents record grants of Attic citizenship
to one of the murderers of Phrynichus (410-9 B.C.),[1] to
some scores of metics who helped Thrasybulus restore
the democracy in 403 B.C.,[2] and to Dionysius of
Syracuse (368 B.C.).[3] The manner in which franchise
was broadcasted in the Hellenistic age may be illustrated from several texts. Thus we find that the Phar-
salians enrolled 364 new burgesses by one act (third
century)[4]; similarly Miletus gave franchise to 600
mercenaries, and a piece of land into the bargain (228
B.C.)[5]; Ephesus sold citizen rights to all ex-service men
at the rate of six minæ (297 B.C.)[6]; Dyme made a similar
offer to all free men and sons of free men at one talent
apiece (third century).[7]

προξενία.—The series of texts illustrating this typical Greek institution begins in the sixth century and
from the fourth century extends to a monotonous
length. This gift of προξενία is often coupled with
ἀτελεία, ἀσυλία and other privileges, but documents
of this class tend to become stereotyped. Their chief
interest lies in the wide ramification of friendly inter-
state relations which they reveal. It is not surprising
that Delphi should have issued 133 decrees of προξενία
between 197 and 164 B.C., and that its radius of relations should have extended to Brundisium, Canusium,

---

[1] H—H 74; DS 108.
[2] H—H 80. This interesting text is unfortunately ill preserved. For a
recent restoration, see G. de Sanctis, *Riv. Fil.* 1923 p. 287 ff.
[3] H—H 108; DS 159.
[4] M 306.
[5] *Milet* I pt. 3 Nos. 33-38.
[6] DS 363 l. 9.
[7] DS 531.

and Rome.[1] But similar decrees have been found by the dozen in such relatively unimportant places as Oropus and Hellenistic Miletus,[2] and some unexpected connexions have been disposed by stray documents of this class. Thus Bœotia had representatives at Carthage and Sinope,[3] Chersonesus Taurica at Rhodes[4]; the tiny towns of Acræphiae in Bœotia and Cierium in Thessaly promoted citizens of Rome to be their πρόξενοι,[5] and the short-lived state of Pisa appointed an agent at Sicyon almost in the hour of its birth (364 B.C.).[6]

προμαντεία.—Records of grants of this kind are naturally commonest at Delphi, where the series of them begins in the sixth century. Among the recipients of this privilege we may notice Philip II of Macedon,[7] Alexander's admiral Nearchus,[8] and barbarians like the sons of Cersebleptes of Thrace.[9] In the Hellenistic age προμαντεῖαι were conferred with a lavishness which would have defeated its own end if the recipients had tried to put their privilege to use: not only individuals but entire states received it. On a series of texts from 270 to 220 B.C. thirty-five grants were recorded in honour of none but Arcadians.[10]

Miscellaneous grants.—In addition to the above, various marks of honour were bestowed singly or in combination. Some were purely complimentary, e.g., votes of thanks (ἐπαινέσεις), statues, the ἰσόθεοι τιμαί voted by the Achæan League to Philopœmen,[11] and the altar

---

[1] DS 585.
[2] For typical specimens, see M 207-16 and *Milet* I, pt. 3, nos. 94-119.
[3] DS 179; *S.E.G.* I, 107.   [4] *I.P.E.* IV, 64.
[5] M 234, 303.   [6] H—H 115; DS 171.
[7] DS 221.   [8] DS 266.   [9] DS 195.
[10] *F.D.* III. 1. 12-46.   [11] DS 624.

erected by the Samothracians to king Lysimachus.[1] The rest were, in theory at least, of material value: golden crowns, free board in the πρυτανεῖον, exemption from imposts and reprisals, the right to acquire land (ἔγκτησις) or to graze on the commons (ἐπινομία), and priority in the hearing of suits (προδικία). In many cases the privileges were made hereditary.

The following rough list of benefactors and their services will show how many sidelights on Greek history are thrown by this class of decree.

Politicians of Greek republics.—The documents bear out the statement of Demosthenes that the custom of awarding public honours to statesmen did not arise long before his time. The vote of thanks to Demosthenes himself in the *De Corona*[2] is spurious; but a similar vote on behalf of his colleague Lycurgus (307-6 B.C.), which formerly was only known from a quotation in the *Vitæ X Oratorum*,[3] has been proved genuine by the discovery of a stone containing the same text.[4] Demosthenes' adversary Androtion appears on another inscription as a model Athenian governor on the island of Amorgos (357-6 B.C.).[5] The "Phædrus decree" (*c.* 272 B.C.), in recapitulating the merits of this politician, summarises the entire history of Athenian relations with Macedon from Cassander to Antigonus Gonatas.[6] Of the statesmen of the Achæan League, Philopœmen received a fulsome award of posthumous honours,[7] Polybius a simple vote of thanks.[8] For successful diplomats honours seem to have flowed less freely than one would

---

[1] DS 372.   [2] § 118.   [3] P. 851-2.
[4] DS 326.   [5] H—H 127; DS 193.
[6] H 167; R—G 55; DS 409.   [7] DS 642.
[8] H 201 (at Olympia).   We know from Polybius himself that this was only one of many decrees passed in his honour (Pol. 40, 8, 11; 40, 10, 4).

expect, but two decrees have been preserved which tell triumphantly how a couple of stalwarts from Lampsacus and Teos undertook to enter the lion's den, i.e., the Curia at Rome, in 196 and 167 B.C. respectively, and actually set the lion purring.[1]

Kings and their agents.—Of the numerous records of benefactions by kings the following may serve as specimens: (i) The rulers of the Cimmerian Bosporus repeatedly gave corn largesse to Athens.[2] (ii) Seleucus I and his son Antiochus took a personal interest in the reconstruction of Apollo's temple at Didyma.[3] (iii) The first two Ptolemies substituted a milder sway in the Cyclades for the exactions of Demetrius.[4] (iv) The third and fifth Ptolemies made concessions to the native priests, who collectively acknowledged these benefits in fulsome terms. The inscriptions containing these decrees are the famous trilinguals of Canopus[5] and Rosetta.[6] (v) Attalus II of Pergamum rescued the towns of the Gallipoli peninsula from a Thracian foray. The stone on which this exploit was recorded was excavated by a British soldier a few hours before being killed in action.[7]

The services of the royal officials and agents usually consisted of a good word at court which brought material benefits to the cities issuing the decree. In one instance two officers from Iasus won the ear of Alexander and obtained fresh territory for that town[8]; in

[1] M 529 and 325.
[2] H—H 140; DS 206 (346 B.C.); DS370 (289 B.C.); cf. also H. 157; DS 371.
[3] O.G.I. 213.
[4] DS 390.
[5] H. 179 (in brief); M 551 (in full).
[6] B.M. 1065; O.G.I. 90.
[7] C.Q. 1917 p. 1.
[8] H—H 165; DS 307.

another the comic poet Philippides induced the miserly king Lysimachus to send corn gratis to Athens.[1] In one text the Athenian Ecclesia thanks a courtier for tuning king Cassander (299-88 c.),[2] elsewhere commanders of royal garrisons are complimented for not abusing their position.[3]

Roman commissioners.—The preponderance of Rome in Greek politics after the battle of Cynoscephalæ is illustrated by a long string of votes to Roman personages, thanking them for favours received or expected. The list of men honoured includes T. Flamininus,[4] P. Scipio,[5] Aemilius Lepidus,[6] Marcius Philippus[7] and L. Mummius.[8]

Arbitrators.—A large and interesting group of documents stands in honour of arbitrators who had composed disputes, internal and inter-state. These votes were sometimes passed by the state which provided the judges, but more usually by the recipients of the award. Thus (i) Delphi honoured nine Rhodian judges who finally delimited the state's frontiers and thus removed a long-standing cause of dispute (*c.* 180 B.C.).[9] (ii) Thespiæ commended one of its citizens for allaying internal disputes at Delphi.[10] (iii) Laodicea praised an umpire from Priene for deciding cases according to the laws of the appellant city—an unusual feat.[11] A notable collection of twenty-four ἐπαινέσεις from Delphi re-

[1] H 160; R—G 52; DS 374.
[2] R—G 51; DS 362.
[3] *E.g. Priene* 21-22 (270-262 B.C.); DS 331 (Megara, 306 B.C.); H 189, M 340 (Ægina, 2nd century).
[4] H 191 (Gythium) DS 616 (Delphi).
[5] As πρόξενος of Delos.   DS 617.   [6] *S.E.G.* I. 147 (Delphi).
[7] DS 649 (Achæan League).
[8] DS 676 (Elis).   [9] DS 614.
[10] *S.E.G.* I. 132.   [11] *Priene* 59.

cords a series of interventions by foreign arbitrators in the disputes of this town. No less than thirteen cases out of this group were heard in 167 B.C. or soon after.[1]

Generous donors.—The list of these is almost endless. The good works thus acknowledged include the building of a stone bridge on the road to Eleusis,[2] the salvaging of shipwrecked sailors,[3] the ransoming of seafearers from pirates.[4] Traders are honoured for free gifts of corn in a time of scarcity,[5] or merely for not causing an artificial dearth,[6] and Roman usurers are thanked for charging low rates and remitting arrears.[7] A Samian inscription commemorates the repayment by a patriotic citizen of debts due to reckless municipal trading,[8] and the famous "Protogenes decree" from Olbia records how a wealthy benefactor again and again redeemed the city from bankruptcy.[9] Resolutions by Attic tribes in favour of generous choregi have been preserved in smaller numbers than might have been expected.[10]

Professional workers.—Aristotle and his nephew Callisthenes received thanks at Delphi for compiling the list of Pythian victors.[11] Other Delphian documents record decrees in honour of poets who had composed hymns and epics for the Pythian festival,[12] for a troup of actors from Athens,[13] for a performer on a water-organ ($\H{v}\delta\rho\alpha\upsilon\lambda o s$),[14] and for two lady musicians ($\chi o\rho o\psi\acute{a}\lambda\tau\rho\iota\alpha\iota$).[15] At Lamia[16] and Chalcion[17] homage

---

[1] *Klio* 1923, p. 268 ff. 5   [2] M 148   [3] DS 341.
[4] H 186; M 384.   [5] R—G 45; DS 304.   [6] DS 640.
[7] H 204 (Tenos); DS 748 (Gythium).   [8] *S.E.G.* I. 366.
[9] DS 495.   [10] *I.G.* II. 554-7.   [11] DS 275.
[12] DS 447-52.   [13] DS 399; *cf.* DS 698.   [14] DS 737.
[15] DS 689, 738. Votes in honour of musicians are not infrequent. *Cf.* DS 703 (Delphi); *S.E.G.* II. 184 (Tanagra).
[16] M 296.   [17] *S.E.G.* II. 263.

was paid to lady poets who had redeemed those towns from obscurity. At Delos ἐπαινέσεις were bestowed on a meritorious school teacher[1] and on a wandering scholar who had made a collection of the local legends.[2] Medical practitioners figure on a notable number of inscriptions. Most of them were visiting doctors from ·other towns who treated the population *en masse* and in many cases refused payment.[3] Lamia complimented a veterinary doctor (ἱππίατρος),[4] and Ilium thanked the court physician of Antiochus I for curing that monarch.[5]

Miscellaneous.—The list of benefactors may be concluded with the following mixed assortment; members of the Athenian Boule[6]; the Prytaneis at Ptolemais in Upper Egypt, who had suppressed local riots[7]; cornwardens[8]; hydraulic engineers[9]; commissioners for public festivals[10]; ephors of Spartan "obes" or parishes[11]; ephebi who had behaved nicely[12]; Athenian maidens who had woven Athena's new πέπλος.[13]

Unclassified decrees. The following further texts deserve mention:

(i) A motion by the orator Lycurgus, that leave be given to Cyprian merchants to set up a temple of Aphrodite, "on the same terms as were accorded to the Egyptians for their temple of Isis."[14]

(ii) An order by the Ecclesia of Gortyn to supply a visiting doctor from Tralles with iron probes, cathartics, wine from Andros, etc. (*c.* 400 B.C.).[15]

(iii) A decree by a new colony of the Adriatic island

[1] M 164.   [2] *B.M.* 364; DS 335, 538, 620.   [3] DS 382.
[4] M 297.   [5] M 526.   [6] R—G 56.
[7] *O.G.I.* 48.   [8] M 482.   [9] M 105.
[10] M 108.   [11] M 182.   [12] R—G 53, 75.
[13] *B.S.A.* XXI. p. 155 ff.   [14] R—G 43; DS 280.   [15] *S.E.G.* I, 414.

of Issa, reserving choice plots of vineland for the first-comers and earmarking the inferior land for later arrivals (early fourth century).[1]

(iv) A resolution by Tomi (in Roumania) to dispense with mercenaries and set up a civic guard of forty men to watch the gates and patrol the town (second century).[2]

(v) An enfranchisement act by the Ecclesia of Pergamum, following upon a posthumous grant of municipal liberty by Attalus III, as announced in the late king's will.[3] This decree proves against critics ancient and modern that the will in question was not a forgery.

[1] DS 141. [2] M 334. [3] *Pergamon* 249.

CHAPTER IV

DECREES RELATING TO FOREIGN AFFAIRS

IN this chapter we shall consider those acts which illustrate the relations between one Greek state and another.

(1) *Alliances.*—The surviving texts mostly stand on stones, but some important documents have been reproduced by historical authors.

Our earliest extant specimen is a badly preserved inscription from the Argive Heræum (*c.* 600 B.C.), which appears to bind Argos, Mycenæ, and Tiryns to take common action against "contrivers of death and any other evil."[1] Two bronze tablets of the sixth or early fifth century from Olympia contain records of alliances for 50 and 100 years respectively, whose infraction was to be penalised as an offence against Zeus Olympius. The contracting parties in the one case were two unnamed states of N.W. Greece,[2] in the other Elis and Heræa.[3]

The diplomatic activities of Pericles are illustrated by a series of texts that record alliances in widely different regions. An inscription of 453-2 B.C. is evidence of a compact between Athens and Egesta[4]; another of 448 B.C. proves a connexion with Phocis[5]; a pair of documents of 433-2 B.C. gives the terms of alliances

---

[1] *A.J.A.* 1901, p. 159.   [2] M 2.   [3] H—H 9; DS 9.
[4] *I.G.* I² 19.   [5] *I.G.* I² 26.

with Rhegium and Leontini which probably repeated those of previous negotiations in 446-40 B.C.[1] The tangled relations between Athens and the powers of the Macedonian seaboard and interior are illustrated by successive diplomatic deals with Philip of Eordæa (432 B.C.),[2] with his rival Perdiccas (423-2),[3] and with the Bottiæi (c. 421 B.C.).[4] The diplomatic cross-currents of Greek politics in 421-417 B.C. are exemplified by three documents: (i) the still-born alliance between Athens and Sparta immediately after Nicias' Peace[5]; (ii) the league with Argos, Mantineia, and Elis by means of which Athens retaliated upon Sparta for breaking the previous pact (420 B.C.)[6]; and a separate Athenian engagement with Argos in 417-6 B.C.[7] The second of these compacts is preserved both in Thucydides and (in part) on an inscription: the two texts differ somewhat in their wording, but they agree in all essentials and thus confirm rather than impair Thucydides' reputation for accuracy. Of the pacts by which Sparta bound herself to Persia in 412-11 B.C., no less than three have been reproduced by Thucydides.[8] In the first of these Sparta actually conceded "all the lands and cities which the king possesses *and his ancestors* did possess"; in the final contract Sparta merely gave away the Asiatic Greeks.

The large series of texts of fourth-century alliances is eloquent proof of the revived ambitions of Athens. The principal document is the manifesto of 377 B.C., with which the Athenians launched their second maritime

---

[1] *B.M.* 5; H—H 51-2; *I.G.* I² 51-2, and note by the editor.
[2] *I.G.* I² 53.   [3] *I.G.* I² 71.
[4] H—H 68; DS 89.   [5] Thuc. V, 23.
[6] Thuc. V, 47; H—H 69.   [7] *I.G.* I² 96.
[8] Thuc. VIII, 18, 37, 58.

confederacy.[1] The history of this league is an ironical commentary on the painfully strict clauses in this agreement by which Athens bound herself to respect her allies' autonomy. The issue of the manifesto is foreshadowed by some earlier overtures to single states such as Carpathos (*c.* 393 B.C.),[2] and Chios (*c.* 386 B.C.)[3]; its somewhat meagre fruits may be sampled in the subsequent conventions with Chalcis[4] and Corcyra.[5] The diplomatic activities of Athens in other quarters are revealed by compacts with Dionysius I of Syracuse (367 B.C.),[6] with the Arcadians and other Peloponnesians (362-1 B.C.),[7] and with the Thessalian confederation (361-0 B.C.),[8] all of which fell through before the stones on which they were engraved had begun to weather.

Another failure, but a highly honourable one, of Athenian diplomacy is recorded in "Chremonides' decree" of 266 B.C., which sounds like the last trumpet-call for a crusade against Macedon.[9] In this document Sparta and other Peloponnesians figure as formal allies of Athens, but the king of Egypt, though the prime mover in this league, assumes the part of an uncovenanted friend.

Of the numerous other alliances of the Hellenistic period whose texts we possess the following deserve mention: (i) A compact between Ætolia and Acarnania

---

[1] H—H 101; DS 147.
[2] H—H 93; DS 129.   [3] H—H 98; DS 142.
[4] H—H 102; DS 148.   [5] H—H 106; DS 151.
[6] H—H 112; DS 163.
[7] H—H 119; DS 181. This inscription gives the name of the prytany during which the alliance was concluded, but does not indicate in which part of the calendar year it fell (as is done in H—H 112). Consequently it is uncertain whether the alliance came before or after the battle of Mantinea.
[8] H—H 123; DS 184.   [9] H 169; R—G 57; DS 434-5.

(*c.* 270 B.C.), which gives valuable information as to rates of pay and rationing in a Greek expeditionary force.[1] (ii) An engagement between Rhodes and the Cretan town of Hierapytna (*c.* 200 B.C.), whose main object was to secure for Rhodes a ready supply of mercenaries and to set one Cretan pirate to catch another.[2] The excellent drafting of this document betrays a Rhodian hand. (iii) The agreement made in 214 B.C. between Philip V of Macedon and Hannibal. In this remarkable pact the contracting parties agree to win the Second Punic War, to exclude the Romans from the Adriatic, and to stand watch for ever over them.[3] (iv) A *fœdus æquum* between omnipotent Rome and the insignificant islet of Astypalæa, in which either party undertakes to mobilise all its horses and all its men in support of the other (105 B.C.).[4]

(2) *Treaties.*—These are the documents which historians most often reproduced verbatim. The earliest extant text, that of the convention between Athens and Chalcis in 446/5 B.C., can still be read on a finely preserved stone.[5] From Thucydides we have the wording of Nicias' two instruments, the armistice of 423 B.C.[6] and the peace of 421 B.C.,[7] and the two successive drafts of the terms on which Sparta and Argos came to an agreement in 418 B.C.[8] The armistice of 423 B.C. is shown by its formulation to be a composite act, to which the Spartans and their allies contributed the terms of settlement, while the Athenians appended the date of its inception and other consequential detail. On the other hand the peace of 421 B.C. was of uniform workman-

[1] DS 421.　　　　　[2] M 21.　　　　　[3] Polybius VII, 9.
[4] H 203.　　　　　[5] H—H 40; DS 64.　　[6] Thuc. IV, 118.
[7] Thuc. V, 18.　　　[8] Thuc. V, 77, 79.

ship. Both instruments were carefully drafted, and the second was at great pains to define the position of the towns on the Thracian sector, on which, as it happened, both settlements broke down.

While the text of Nicias' peace occupies some sixty lines, the peace that ended the Peloponnesian War is a Laconic instrument in more senses than one: "demolish Piræus and the Long Walls; evacuate all the cities; keep your own land; do that and you may have peace; you must pay your dues and recall your exiles; as to the number of your ships, you must do what they (i.e., the ephors) decide."[1] Of the notorious King's Peace of 386 B.C. Xenophon has preserved the most characteristic clauses: "King Artaxerxes deems it right that the cities in Asia should be his . . . and that the other Greek cities, great and small, should be autonomous . . . whichever party refuses this peace I shall, with the help of those who accept, coerce by land and sea, with ships and money."[2] From Polybius we have the texts of three treaties imposed upon Greek states by the Romans. (i) The Peace of Flamininus (196 B.C.), which opened with a general proclamation of freedom for the Greeks of Europe and Asia, and actually secured this freedom against Philip V of Macedon.[3] (ii) The terms accorded in 189 B.C. to Antiochus III of Syria. These are given by Polybius both in the interim form sketched out by Scipio and in the final draft as elaborated by Cn. Manlius.[4] (iii) The collateral treaty between Rome and the Ætolians, a document quite long enough to have flattered the losers' sense of their own importance.[5] We

[1] Plutarch, *Lysander*, Ch. 14. [2] *Hellenica* V, 1, 31.
[3] Polyb. XVIII. 44. [4] Polyb. XXI, 14, XXII. 23.
[5] Polyb. XXII, 13.

may conclude this series with an extraordinary compact made by Eumenes I of Pergamum with some of his mutinous mercenaries (263 B.C.).[1] In effect, Eumenes capitulated to his troops and promised not only an indemnity, but a fixed scale of deductions from pay for bread and wine, and contributions to the invalid, pensions, and orphan funds. This agreement was to be confirmed by an exchange of oaths and exhibited in four different places.

(3) *Affiliations of colonies to mother-states.*—During the principal period of Greek colonisation no legal ties bound parent and daughter city together, and no documents survive to illustrate their relations. From the fifth century we have a law prescribing the mutual rights and duties of the Opuntian Locrians and their colonists at Naupactus.[2] Opus conceded a privileged position to the Naupactians in her own courts, and allowed them, as Rome allowed her Latin colonists, to resume their former franchise under certain conditions. These terms, we may suspect, were not repeated in other cases where the colonists were separated from their former home by a long distance.

Two inscriptions of the age of Alexander throw light on the relations between Miletus and her daughter cities. In one of these Miletus exchanges *ius commercii* and *ius honorum* with Olbia,[3] in the other it is stipulated that "a citizen of Cyzicus shall be a Milesian at Miletus" and vice versa.[4]

The procedure followed by Athens in founding colonies is made known by two inscriptions respecting Brea

[1] *O.G.I.* 266.   [2] H—H 25; *B.M.* 954.
[3] DS 286.
[4] *Milet* I pt. 3, no. 137.

in Thrace (*c.* 446-5 B.C.)[1] and a settlement somewhere
on the Adriatic coast (325-4 B.C.).[2] The colony at Brea
was confined to the poorer citizen classes; the details
of settlement were left over to an "autocrat" commissioner. The Adriatic post seems to have been regarded
as a place of exile rather than a new home, for elaborate
provision had to be made to ensure that immigrants
should take up their allotments. From the sixth-century
decree concerning Salamis we must forbear to draw
conclusions, for its text and its date remain uncertain.[3]
From two fragmentary decrees regarding the cleruchy
at Hestiæa (after 446-5 B.C.)[4] we can at least infer that
the settlers only enjoyed limited rights of jurisdiction
even in civil suits, and that they were liable to εἰσφορά
or property tax.

(4) *Resolutions of the Athenians concerning their subject-
allies.*—T ̣ ⸱ constitution imposed upon Erythræ has
already been noticed (Ch. II, p. 15). The capitulations
accorded to Chalcis (446-5 B.C.)[5] and Ceos (363-2 B.C.)[6]
afford good instances of the manner in which Athens
dealt with rebellion. The ringleaders are outlawed or
committed to trial, but in the latter case they are assured
of a regular hearing, and a general pardon is proclaimed
for all others.

Examples of commercial restrictions imposed by the
Athenians are few but instructive. On an inscription of
426 B.C. we read of a special permit given to Methone
in Macedonia to import corn from Byzantium, which
is proof of a general embargo upon such trade.[7] The

---

[1] H—H 41; DS 67.   [2] DS 305.   [3] H—H 4; *I.G.* I² 1.
[4] *I.G.* I² 40-41 and 42; M. Cary, *J.H.S.* 1925, p. 243 ff.
[5] H—H 40; DS 64.   [6] H—H 118; DS 173.
[7] H—H 60 (2nd decree) § 1; DS 75.

"despot's progress" is marked by a drastic decree of
c. 420 B.C., by which a monopoly of coinage was set up
on behalf of the Athenian mint.[1] Copies of this decree
were ordered to be set up in all the allied states. The
resumption of a restrictive policy under the second
confederacy is marked by decrees of the three towns on
Ceos, which bind all dealers in red ochre, the staple
product of the island, to export only to Piræus.[2]

(5) *Affederations and amalgamations.*—Apart from the
special treaties of alliance by means of which the Athenians enrolled new members into their second confederacy (see pp. 37-8), we possess little documentary evidence
on the process of affederation. The act by which the
Achæan League enrolled Arcadian Orchomenus is
partly preserved on a stone, but all the important clauses
are missing.[3] A resolution of the Delphian Amphictyony by which an application for membership on the
part of Messene and Megalopolis is referred to the
constituent states (c. 346 B.C.)[4] tells us nothing that
might not have been easily guessed.

Of acts relating to συνοικισμοί or fusions of two
cities into one, we have a specimen in a decree of the
Ætolian League respecting the small towns of Stiris
and Medeon (c. 175 B.C.).[5] The details preserved relate
mainly to the judicial and constitutional arrangements
involved by this amalgamation. A similar inscription
relating to the incorporation of Lebedus in Teos will be
discussed in Ch. VII (p. 74).

---

[1] DS 87; *Zeitschrift für Numismatik*, 1925, p. 217.
[2] H—H 137; M 401.
[3] H 187; DS 490.
   [4] Didymus col. 6, l. 1. The enrolment of Magnesia in the Amphictyony
in c. 208 B.C. was purely honorary (DS 554).
   [5] DS 647.

The conferment of a city's franchise upon the citizens of another state *en bloc* (συμπολιτεία) is recorded in two Attic documents, the former of which relates to the refugees from Platæa in 427 B.C.,¹ the latter to the Samians after the battle of Ægospotami (405 B.C.).² The Platæans were disqualified from holding an archonship or entering a phratry; the Samians were placed under no special disabilities. From Smyrna we have an almost interminable inscription which sets forth in profuse detail the terms of enfranchisement for an adjacent military colony of Seleucus II (*c.* 240 B.C.).³

The interchange of franchise between two cities (ἰσοπολιτεία) is regulated with minute detail in an extant treaty between the Cretan towns of Hierapytna and Priansium (third century). By this act each city receives the freedom of the other's lands and markets, the chief magistrates of either place attend the Ecclesia of the other, and mutual disputes are referred to a mixed tribunal.⁴ Similar arrangements between Miletus and her colonies have been noted on p. 41.

(6) ἀσφαλεία *and* ἀσυλία.—A form of inter-state agreement which became common in the Hellenistic age was a guarantee against plunder and blackmail. Originally such guarantees were only given to sacred places like Olympia and Delphi⁵; eventually many of the more defenceless cities secured like privileges. A remarkable series of treaties of third century date by which the Ætolian League offered to restrain its soldatesca from their usual acts of pillage has survived on

¹ [Dem.] 59 § 104.   ² H—H 81 § 2; DS 116.
³ H 176; O.G.I. 229.   ⁴ H 172; M 16.
⁵ *Cf.* M 700; a guarantee of personal security given by the Delphic Amphictyony to pilgrims on the way to the Bœotian shrine of Apollo Ptoïus.

inscriptions. The recipients include Delos,[1] Ceos,[2] Chios,[3] Mytilene[4] and Magnesia-on-Mæander.[5]

(7) *Commercial treaties.* The earliest form of mercantile pact in Greece was probably an arrangement by which states agreed to prevent the primitive practice of σύλη in the commercial sense, i.e., indiscriminate distraint for debt, and to provide courts at which alien creditors might enforce their claims. One such contract, inscribed in letters of fifth-century form but drafted with archaic clumsiness, regulates the relations of Œanthea and Chaleum, two tiny towns of western Locris, on these lines.[6] A much more advanced type of treaty is preserved on a stone, probably of *c.* 450 B.C., in which the states of Athens and Phaselis agree to provide courts for various kinds of commercial claims.[7] Unfortunately many of the readings on this stone are uncertain.

Several fourth-century treaties conceding most-favoured-nation treatment have come down to us. One of these, by which King Leucon of the Cimmerian Bosporus lowered his dues on exported corn in favour of Mytilene, was no doubt a wholly amicable agreement (*c.* 350 B.C.).[8] On the other hand, the permission to export timber free of charge which Amyntas III of Macedon gave to the Chalcidian League was probably extorted under duress.[9] The second of these inscriptions shows that commercial Greek, like commercial English, could soar high above the rules of grammar. The opening up of trade which followed upon Alex-

[1] *I.G.* XI, 4, 1050 (*c.* 250 B.C.).   [2] H 178; DS 522.   [3] DS 443.   [4] M 25.
[5] DS 554.   [6] H—H 44; B.M. 953.
[7] H—H 36.; 'Εφ. 'Αρχ. 1922, p. 62 ff.
[8] DS 212.   [9] H—H 95; DS 135.

ander's Anabasis is illustrated by a treaty between Miletus and Sardes in which either party agreed not to molest the merchants of the other.[1] A curious document of *c.* 390 B.C. contains the renewal of a compact between Mytilene and Phocæa by which these two states agreed to co-operate in the emission of coins and to issue no "diluted" (ὑδαρέστερον) money.[2] According to numismatists the second of these resolves was made none too soon.[3] Another strange agreement, of similar date, was made between the Cretan town of Præsus and some smaller neighbours, who received certain fishing rights on condition that they should find provisions for coasters working the southern shore of Crete.[4]

(8) *Inter-state courtesies.* A form of civility between Greek states which gained considerable vogue in the Hellenistic age was the official invitation of representatives (θεωροί) from other cities to public festivals such as then sprang up like mushrooms and in some cases attained "isolympic" or "isopythic" standing. One such invitation was sent by Miletus to Cos, when the former city promoted its Didymeia to the rank of a panhellenic festival.[5] Another was broadcasted over Greece by the Ætolians when these founded a new Delphic festival, the Soteria, to commemorate the victory of the confederate Greeks over the Gallic invaders of 279 B.C. The replies of two states, Chios and Athens, are still preserved.[6] But the best illustration of this procedure will be found in a complete corpus of inscriptions from Magnesia-on-the-Mæander relating to the foundation of a festival of Artemis Leucophryene (206 B.C.). The

---

[1] *Milet* I, 3. no. 135.   [2] H—H 94; M 8.
[3] P. Gardner, *History of Ancient Coinage*, p. 176.   [4] M 440.
[5] *S. Ber. Berl.* 1905, p. 979 ff.   [6] H 161; DS 402, 408.

first decree contains a manifesto of the Magnesians who quote a Delphic oracle and an epiphany of Artemis to support their plea[1]; on the remaining stones, forty-two in number, we read the friendly replies of states ranging from Epidamnus to Antioch in Persia.[2]

An unusual act of inter-state friendship is commemorated in an inscription of 282 B.C., in which Miletus thanks Cnidus for assistance in paying off a loan to King Lysimachus.[3] Twenty-eight Cnidians subscribed and seventy-five others underwrote the loan. It may be surmised that the hidden hand behind this suspicious display of generosity was that, of Cnidus' overlord, Ptolemy II.

Royal rescripts, which were decrees in substance but not in form, will be dealt with in Ch. VII.

---

[1] *Magn.* 16. [2] *Magn.* 23-64. [3] *Milet* I, pt. 3, no. 138.

CHAPTER V

EXECUTIVE RECORDS

THE executive "acta" of Greek states constitute a large and varied class of documents.

(1) FINANCIAL RECORDS: (a) *Statements of revenue.* (i) *Proceeds of taxation.*—Among the prizes drawn in the excavations on the Athenian Acropolis few were more valuable than the series of stones on which were engraved the payments made by the subject-allies of Athens from 454 to 414 B.C.[1] On these inscriptions the figures entered against each ally denotes not the actual amount of his contribution but a quota of one-sixtieth part thereof, which was made over to Athena as a special fee for receiving the treasures of the Delian League in deposit.[2] But it is a simple matter to compute the full tribute from the quota. Most of the stones are badly broken, but the legible parts of one often serve to restore another, and in the aggregate these records are a rich mine of information regarding the membership of the Delian Confederacy, its regional grouping, and the fluctuations in the tribute imposed upon each ally.

Official receipts for taxes paid by private persons

---

[1] *I.G.* I² 191-231. Representative specimens in H—H 33, 48 (433/2), no 436(5 B.C.), 65. On the whole subject of Attic finances in the fifth century see E. Cavaignac, *Études sur l'histoire financière d'Athènes au 5ème siècle.*

[2] A list of actual sums due to be paid by each ally is appended to the τάξις φόρου of 425/4 B.C. (see p. 25). For this refer to *I.G.* I² 63 rather than to H—H 64, in which τάξεις of different years have been conflated.

haye been found in large quantities in Egypt. For the sake of economy these statements were usually made out, not on papyrus, but on scraps of broken pottery (ὄστρακα), which have survived by the thousand.[1] These ostraca constitute our chief source of knowledge concerning the objects and incidence of Ptolemaic as of Roman taxation in Egypt. Most of the receipts are made out in a set form and have no individual interest. Among those which deserve notice are statements regarding customs dues at the unusual rate of 20–50 per cent.,[2] licence fees paid by money-changers,[3] payments of corn, for the sifting and cleaning of which the government imposed a slight additional tax.[4] One extensive papyrus contains a list of receipts from no less than fifty villages.[5]

(ii) *Fines.*—A small but highly interesting collection of records of this class relates to the payments made by the Phocians from 343 to 324 B.C. for their sacrilege at Delphi.[6] The reduction of the fine from sixty to ten talents per annum, which took place in 337 B.C., no doubt was the result of Philip's moderating influence.

(iii) *Sales.*—Occasional sidelights on politics are thrown by the sale-records of confiscated property. In an early fifth-century text from Halicarnassus we have evidence of a big political upheaval, for the victims are numbered by scores.[7] Among them is one Panyassis,

[1] U. Wilcken's *Griechische Ostraka*, which is the chief text-book on the subject, contains some 1,600 specimens, mostly however of the Roman period. *Cf.* also W. Schubart and E. Kühn, *Papyri und Ostraka der Ptolemäerzeit*, nos. 1304-1456.
[2] *ASA* XXIII, no. 73, p. 74 ff.
[3] P. Viereck, *Griechische und griechisch-demotische Ostraka der Universität und Landesbibliothek zu Strassburg* I, 1-13.
[4] *Lille* I, 20.   [5] P. *Petr.* II, 28.
[6] DS 230-5. One specimen in H—H 141.   [7] DS 46.

possibly the uncle of Herodotus who lost his life in an abortive rising against the tyrant Lygdamis, but the point is uncertain. An Athenian inscription of 414 B.C. schedules the confiscated estates of Alcibiades and of several Hermocopid outlaws.[1] The inventories contain interesting details about slaves and bedroom furniture. On a fourth-century stone from Iasus is a long list of buyers, many of them magistrates and priests, whose official dignity could not resist a cheap bargain.[2] From Egypt we have several auction lists of ἀδέσποτα, i.e., crown-lands escheat on the decease or removal of a life-tenant, usually a Greek or Macedonian military pensioner.[3]

A common source of revenue in Greek towns, especially during the Hellenistic age, consisted in the sale of priesthoods.[4] The price paid for simony varied greatly according to the prestige of each office and its perquisites. At Priene the priesthood of Poseidon fetched 4,000 drachmas, that of Dionysus, 12,000[5]; at Erythræ Ge was rated at ten pieces of silver, Hermes Agoræus at 4,610.[6] With these sales we may couple those of the hides of sacrificial animals (δερματικά), of which we have an inventory from Athens (334–1 B.C.).[7]

(iv) *Registration fees.*—These figure but rarely and only on documents of late date. A good example is provided by an inscription from Melitæa in Phthiotis, which records payments of a uniform fee of fifteen staters for registering the manumission of slaves (first century).[8]

---

[1] H—H 72; DS 96-103.   [2] DS 169.
[3] *P. Petr.* III, 104-5; Schubart-Kühn, 1219-22.
[4] These sales, however, had existed in previous times. See W. Otto *Hermes*, 1911, p. 594.
[5] *Priene* 174; *cf.* 201-3.   [6] DS 1014.
[7] R—G 100.   [8] *I.G.* IX, 2, 206.

(v) *Gifts and loans.*—That characteristic device of Greek finance, the ἐπίδοσις or donation, is often met with on inscriptions: its objects range from the waging of a war to the repair of a bath.[1] On a unique Spartan στήλη stands a list of contributions in money and kind towards the costs of the Peloponnesian War (428-1 B.C.).[2] Two stones at Delphi record the benevolences that poured in from all Hellenedom for rebuilding Apollo's temple (369 B.C. ff.).[3] A less widespread enthusiasm is revealed by a list of donations which the Bœotians collected for the Sacred War: the funds came mostly from Byzantium and N.W. Greece.[4] The scale of payments varies greatly: at the small town of Erythræ we find one man giving the services of 500 stonemasons (c. 300 B.C.)[5]; at Athens we meet with a flat rate of 200 drachmas (230–28 B.C.).[6]

Documents relating to income from loans are rarer than the frequency of such loans suggests. A good specimen will be found in an inscription from Carystus, which schedules a long tale of borrowings from citizens of Thebes and Histiæa.[7]

(*b*) *Statements of expenditure.*—The most important records that fall under this head come from Athens. A running commentary on Thucydides is furnished by the statements of sums borrowed by the Hellenotamiæ or the Strategi from the funded treasures on the Acropolis.[8] By means of these entries we can gauge the scale of various field operations and appraise more accurately

---

[1] For the bath, see E. Kalinka, *Tituli Asiæ Minoris* II, pt. 1, no. 168.
[2] DS 84.   [3] DS 239-40.   [4] DS 201.
[5] *Abh. Berl. Ak.* 1909. Paper on *Nordionische Steine*, p. 19, no. 5.
[6] R—G 59.   [7] *I.G.* XII. 9, 7.
[8] *I.G.* I² 293-304 (441-406 B.C.), and 324 (426-2 B.C.). Part of these are reproduced in H—H 53, 62, 70; R—G 99, 109.

the war policy of Athens. The whole history of Pericles' building activity on the Acropolis can be written in the light of the records of expenditure kept by his commissioners of works.[1] The most notable payments are the sums expended on the Parthenon (447–33 B.C.)[2] and the statue of Athena̧ (447–33 B.C.)[3] on the Propylæa (437–3 B.C.),[4] and the costs of resumed construction on the Erechtheum (409–6 B.C.).[5]

The last-named are set forth in great detail in the famous "Chandler inscription," which is also a main source of information for the organisation of the building industry at Athens and the workmen's rates of pay. On a similar long text of 329–8 B.C. we can study the expenditure on Lycurgus' constructions at Eleusis,[6] where the prices of materials and the wages were half as high again as those of the Chandler inscription. Some details about the refortification of Athens and Piræus in the fourth century may be derived from a few fragments of building records. The upper courses were built, as in the fifth century walls, of sun-dried brick. In 394-3 B.C. Megarian and Bœotian contractors lent a hand in the rebuilding of the Long Walls.[7]

Some notable records of expenditure on buildings survive from other parts of Greece. A long inscription from Epidaurus illustrates point for point the work on the Asclepieum (early fourth century),[8] and a series of records from Miletus throws light on the recon-

---

[1] See W. B. Dinsmoor, *A.J.A.* 1913 and 1921.
[2] *I.G.* I² 339-53; H—H 47.   [3] *I.G.* I² 354-62.
[4] *Ibid.* 363-7.   [5] *Ibid.* 372-4; M 571-3; B.M. 35.
[6] M 581.
[7] H—H 90; *A.M.* 1905, p. 391 ff. On the whole subject, see A. Frickenhaus, *Athens Mauern im IVten Jahrhundert v. Chr.* For the Long Walls of Pericles we have only literary evidence.
[8] M 584.

struction of the temple at Didyma (early third century).[1] The quarrying and mason's work at this last site was performed by ἱεροὶ παῖδες, i.e., temple slaves, not the usual hired labourers.

From Egypt we have numerous documents relating to petty routine expenditure, pay for troopers,[2] fodder for their mounts,[3] wages of indented cloth-workers[4] and of diggers engaged on dyke construction,[5] freightage for cargoes of bricks,[6] seed-corn for crown tenants.[7]

Repayments of municipal loans are recorded on two instructive documents, both apparently of the third century. In one of these Bœotian Orchomenus records a settlement with a creditor named Eubolus, who received into the bargain four years' grazing rights on the town commons.[8] In the other the same town after much haggling and threats of distraint paid in full one Nicareta of Thespiæ.[9]

An isolated item of interest occurs in a list of payments for sacrificial animals at Erythræ, early in the second century. The deities to whom these victims were offered included both Rome and Antiochus III.[10] Thus did Erythræ back the whole field.

(c) *Accounts.*—Statements in which expenditure is balanced against revenue are plentiful, thanks to the great hauls of documents of this class at Delphi and Delos. The temple finance of Delphi for the period 360–319 B.C. is summarised in two long series of in-

---

[1] *Rev. Phil.* 1905, p. 237 ff.; 1925 p. 5 ff.; *S-Ber. Berl.* 1911, p. 59 ff.
[2] *P. Strassburg* II, 103-8.
[3] *P. Petr.* II, 25, III, 61.   [4] *P. Hibeh* I, 67.
[5] *P. Petr.* III, 37.
[6] *P. Petr.* II, 14, III, 46.   [7] Schubart-Kühn 1226-30. *Cf. P. Petr.* III, 63 (a bank's pay-day lists).
[8] *B.M.* 158; M 1362.   [9] *I.J.G.* I.1 4.
[10] *Abh. Berl. Ak.* 1909. Paper on *Nordionische Steine,* p. 48.

scriptions, the accounts of the commissioners for the reconstruction of Apollo's shrine (ναοποιόι), and of a board of treasurers (ταμίαι) who partly relieved the ναοποιόι from 339 to 323 B.C.[1] The ναοποιόι kept three separate sets of entries for the funds accruing from the city of Delphi, from the Phocian fines, and from Panhellenic contributions. But valuable as these documents are, they are surpassed by the unique collection of texts from Delos. To say nothing of two isolated inscriptions from the earlier period of Athenian predominance, which embrace the years 434–2 and 377–3 B.C.,[2] we possess a series of stones which all but cover the years 315–166 B.C.[3] Moreover the Delian accounts are made out with a great wealth of detail. Taking for instance the excellently preserved record for 279 B.C.,[4] we find on the revenue side rents of land and houses, interest on loans to cities and private persons, tithes, customs, fishery dues, sales of a tamarisk stump and of a dead goose; on the expenditure side building materials of all kinds, and payments to masons, carpenters, clerks, lady flautists, etc. From these inscriptions some instructive price curves and wage statistics have been derived.[5]

Secular finance is not so well illustrated by records of this kind. The longest text is a first-century inscription from Tauromenium which contains a series of departmental accounts reckoned in copper talents, and

[1] DS 241-8, 249-53.
[2] H—H 50 and 104.
[3] *I.G.* XI, 2, 135-289.
[4] M 594.
[5] G. Glotz, *Journal des Savans*, 1913, p. 16 ff., 206 ff., 251 ff. and *Revue des études grecques*, 1916, p. 281 ff.; J. Bury, *The Hellenistic Age*, Ch. iv (by W. Tarn).

statements of balances, on permanent deposit or at short call, at two private banks.[1]

(2) RECORDS OF PROPERTY. (*a*) *Temple inventories.* — The dedications in the temple of Athena Polias, the Hecatompedus and the Parthenon were invoiced year by year, and of these catalogues a continuous series from 434 to 407 B.C. has survived.[2] Well-preserved lists have also come down to us from Delos, Samos, and Miletus.[3] The items on these lists are usually enumerated row by row, and the weight of objects in precious metal is appended. The treasures include cast-offs and objects of merely symbolical value, but the majority are of gold and silver, mostly in the form of cups.

(*b*) *Naval inventories.* — From Athens we possess a series of "navy lists" from 373 to 322 B.C. These important documents contain schedules of warships and their tackle, which are of the greatest value for the history of the Athenian war-fleet, and as sources of information concerning the technique of ancient navigation.[4]

(*c*) *Land surveys.* — These were in some instances embodied in public leases (see Ch. III, pp. 25–6). The nearest approach to a Greek Domesday is in a second-century papyrus from Memphis, in which the following details are noted: (i) situation, (ii) legal category of each plot, ($\gamma\hat{\eta}$ $\beta\alpha\sigma\iota\lambda\iota\kappa\dot{\eta}$, $\kappa\lambda\hat{\eta}\rho\sigma\varsigma$, etc.), (iii) crops sown, (iv) class of labour employed ($\gamma\epsilon\omega\rho\gamma\dot{\sigma}\varsigma$ $\alpha\dot{\upsilon}\tau\dot{\sigma}\varsigma$, etc.).[5] Another Egyptian survey, prefixed to a scheme of improvements on a latifundium leased by Ptolemy II

[1] DS 954. [2] *I.G.* I² 232-92; R—G 103-5. [3] M 811-23, 832-3, 836-8.
[4] *I.G.* II, 789-812; R—G 119-120; M 601-2, 604. For recent discussions of the subject, see W. Kolbe, *A.M.* 1901 p. 377 ff.; B. Keil, *Anonymus Argentinensis*, Appendix.
[5] Schubart-Kühn 1216.

to his finance minister Apollonius, also deserves mention.[1]

The organisation of the mining industry at Laurium is illustrated by the registers of workings taken over by private entrepreneurs.[2] These contain the names of the lessees, a description of the working (whether new or old), and a careful delimitation of its site.

(d) *Assessments and estimates.*—Information about agricultural life in Egypt may be gleaned from papyri containing measurements of task-work on dykes and canals,[3] and estimates of prospective crops on the domain land.[4] In this connexion we may also draw attention to a large class of property assessments by tenant cultivators under the Ptolemies, which throw some light on labour conditions in Egypt.[5]

(e) *Boundary stones.*—These have been recovered in large numbers, especially on temple precincts. The following are worthy of note: (i) Four stones of the early fifth century at Athens, which delimit the fall-in grounds of Athenian trittyes (battalions).[6] (ii) A fifth-century bourne at Samos, whose legend (ὅρος τεμένους Ἀθηναίας Ἀθηνῶν μεδεούσης) suggests a confiscation of land by the Athenians, probably in 439 B.C.[7] (iii) A line of stones which marked off the territories of Priene and Magnesia according to an arbitral decision (c. 190 B.C.).[8] To this list may be added a stone at

---

[1] *P. Lille* I, 1.

[2] R—G 112; DS 1202-3. On the whole subject of the διαγραφαὶ μετάλλων, see E. Ardaillon, *Les mines du Laurion*, Ch. viii.

[3] *P. Petr.* III, Appendix.   [4] *P. Petr.* III, 95-102.

[5] *Chrest.* I, 198 (an occupier makes a return of 13 slaves and 8 hired workers).

[6] R—G 338-40; DS 917-20.   [7] *S.E.G.* I, 375.

[8] *Priene* 151-5. *Cf.* also the stones on the boundary of Laconia and Messenia which belong to the final delimitation in 78 A.D. (DS 935.)

Thermopylae inscribed "φιλίππου τετραρχίας ἔργον."[1] This indicates that Philip II of Macedon had a force engaged on fortification works at this spot, perhaps in 339–8 B.C.

(f) *Miscellaneous.*—The following also deserve mention: (i) Ptolemaic catalogues of cavalry mounts, described as roans, bays, etc.[2] (ii) The time-book of a Ptolemaic postal transit office, from which the daily movements of the government express post can be reconstructed.[3] (iii) Government wall-tiles from Sparta and Pergamum, inscribed δαμόσιος τειχέων, βασιλικὴ κεραμίς, etc.[4] (iv) Corn jars from Crimea, with the legend βασιλικὴ Σπαρτόκου, etc.[5] (v) Medicine vases stamped with the public seal and name of the eponymous στεφανηφόρος at Priene.[6]

(3) RECORDS OF PERSONS. (a) *Military registers.*—Catalogues of ephebi undergoing military training become fairly common from the fourth century onward. The longest series, of third-century date, comes from Bœotia and Megaris.[7] On these stones it is usually stated that the year-class in question was drafted to some regiment on completion of its exercises.

The most interesting of the military documents are the lists of men fallen in war. These mostly belong to the fifth century, at which time mercenaries had not yet displaced citizen levies. The following may serve as instances: (i) The "Erechtheis" inscription of 459-8 B.C., containing the names of 168 Athenians, all of the

---

[1] DS 220. [2] *P. Petr*, II, 35.
[3] F. Preisigke, *Klio* VII, p. 241 ff.
[4] *B.S.A.* XIII, p. 17 ff.; *Pergamon* 641-51.
[5] E. Pridik, *Amphora Stamps*, p. 129 (text in Russian).
[6] *Priene*, 356.
[7] M 618-39. For an Athenian list of 334 B.C., see M 603.

Erechtheis tribe, who fell in six different theatres of war—an excessive strain upon Athenian man-power.[1] (ii) Twenty-seven soldiers from Cleonæ in Argolis, who assisted the Athenians at Tanagra (457 B.C.).[2] (iii) Fifty-eight Athenians who were killed on the Gallipoli peninsula and at Byzantium (c. 440 B.C.).[3] (iv) A composite list of seventy-seven Athenians, metics and mercenaries, most of whom probably lost their lives at Delium (424 B.C.).[4] (v) Ninety-seven Thespians, who presumably died in the same battle.[5] An Olympian and a Pythian winner are included among these. (vi) Two Athenian strategi and a large but uncertain number of men who fell in the campaign of 394 B.C.[6]

From Nymphæum in S. Russia we have a third-century list which does not state its purpose but probably is a register of men available for military duty.[7] It is noteworthy that all but a very few names on this list are purely Greek.

(b) *Taxation lists.*—Some good specimens of these have been found in Egypt. One typical schedule contains the names of tenants on the crown domain in one district, together with details of rents and taxes due from them.[8] Another catalogue classifies the inhabitants of a village by their callings: six money-changers and nine φῶρες (searchers?) are entered.[9] From Ilium and Erythræ we have extensive registers which do not explain their object but may be taken for schedules of citizens qualified for receiving public doles.[10] In this class we may also include a list of eighty-four enemies of Rome

---

[1] H—H 26; R—G 359.   [2] H—H 28; M 611.   [3] H—H 46; R—G 361.
[4] B.M. 38; DS 77.   [5] M 616.   [6] R—G 362; A.M. 1910, p. 219.
[7] I.P.E. IV, 205.   [8] P. Tebt. I, 93.   [9] P. Petr. III, 59.
[10] M 667; Ἐφ. Ἀρχ. 1911, p. 9.

who were expelled in 189-8 B.C., and had their estates confiscated.[1]

(c) *Lists of officials.*—Catalogues of state-magistrates are comparatively rare. From Athens we have registers of arbitrators (διαιτηταί) who had received a crown for public services,[2] and of πρυτάνεις[3] and βουλευταί' of the fourth century, who had been similarly honoured.[4] The catalogues of ναοποιοί from Delphi (346 B.C. ff.) are noteworthy because this was an international board to which different states from time to time sent representatives.[5]

Lists of priests on the other hand are numerous and sometimes attain great length. The largest number of names stands on a register of annual αἰσυμνῆται τῶν μολπῶν at Miletus, which stretches with scarcely a gap from 525 B.C. to A.D. 32, and suffers no break after the Ionian Revolt.[6] The longest span of time is measured in a catalogue of life-long priests of Poseidon at Halicarnassus, which begins with a mythical son of the god and extends to the first century B.C.[7] From the high-backed seats in the front row of the theatre at Athens we may collect the names of fifty-nine priests who enjoyed προεδρία at the festival of Dionysus. Among these were priests of Hadrian and of "the Demos, the Charites, and Rome"—a strange trinity.[8] Another notable list is that of the priests of some fifty deities at Seleucia in Pieria, including all the kings of Syria down to Antiochus IV.[9] Akin to these lists are two Delphic catalogues of "θεαροδόκοι" who acted as

---

[1] *Klio*, 1920, p. 125 ff., no. 118.
[2] R—G 151
[4] M 1525.
[6] *Milet* I, pt. 3, nos. 122-8.
[8] R—G 247-307; M 860.

[3] R—G 148-9.
[5] DS 237-8.
[7] DS 1020.
[9] *O.G.I.* 245.

hosts to official participants at Apollo's festivals.[1] The
earliest list, of fifth-century date, is incomplete, yet
comprises quite insignificant places in Arcadia and
Macedonia.[2] The later one, of 200–175 B.C., contains
several hundreds of names, grouped in regions after the
fashion of the Athenian tribute lists.[3] From this catalogue it appears that some towns had no less than six
public hosts at their disposal. Lastly, at Olympia there
was found a long series of schedules of the entire staffs
of priests who were not attached to any particular
deity: these include cooks, doctors, clerks, carpenters,
sextons, and so forth.[4]

(4) CALENDARS AND CHRONICLES.—Of ritual calendars, analogous to the original fasti of the Roman
pontifices, we may mention a sixth-century fragment
from Miletus,[5] and an elaborate catalogue of daily
sacrifices at Cos, in which special rites are assigned to
each of the three Doric tribes.[6]

Of extant official chronicles the commonest are
records of competitions at festivals, in which the events,
the winners, and in some cases the prizes, are set forth
in detail. The order of events at the Panathenæa,[7] the
Delia,[8] the Isthmia and Nemea,[9] the Soteria,[10] and many
minor festivals may be reconstructed from surviving
records of proceedings. A continuous catalogue of
winners at the Olympic festival may be drawn up from

---

[1] On the status of θεωροδόκοι, see an inscription from Gonni in Thessaly
which sets forth their privileges at Athens ('Εφ. 'Αρχ. 1914, p. 167).
[2] DS 90. Cf. also the list of Delphic πρόξενοι in DS 585 (2nd century).
[3] B.C.H. 1921, p. 1 ff.; Wiener Anzeiger, 1924, p. 103.
[4] Olymp. 59-141.
[5] Milet I, pt. 3, no. 31. Among the officials mentioned here is a βασιλεύς.
[6] M 716-8.   [7] R—G 169; M 880, 883.
[8] M 902-4.   [9] DS 1057.   [10] M 895.

the annalistic entries in Diodorus' history and the time-tables of Eusebius. Extracts from the Olympic records are also preserved in a papyrus which gives the names of the winners from 480 to 468 B.C. and from 456 to 448 B.C.,[1] and in an unfortunately fragmentary inscription which recounts the dates of inception of each event.[2] A priceless series of documents, if we but had it complete, would be the chronicles of the dramatic contests at Athens. The original records of the archons in charge were collected and classified by Aristotle, and stone copies which were perhaps derived from Aristotle's lists were set up at Athens in the third century. The remaining fragments form part of three lists: (i) the yearly winners in the lyric and dramatic events in the City Dionysia, (ii) the yearly dramatic events in the City Dionysia and the Lenæa, with names of poets and actors, (iii) the total number of prizes won by each poet. Unfortunately we have nothing relating to the classical period of the drama except the entries for 473–1, 459–7 and 423–1 B.C.[3]

Of city and temple chronicles like the "annales" of the Roman pontiffs two short fragments and one document of great length deserve mention. On an inscription from Magnesia part of the foundation-legend of the town is preserved: the "augusta auguria" of its birth included four oracles and a σημεῖον in the shape of a white raven.[4] A sadly mutilated stone from Pergamum contains some stray entries of fourth-century date which formed part of a general history of this

---

[1] *P. Ox.* II, 222.   [2] *I.G.* II, 978.
[3] R—G 170-1, M 879, 881-2, 885. On the whole subject, see Ad. Wilhelm and G. Kaibel, *Urkunden dramatischer Aufführungen in Athen*, and A. E. Haigh, A. W. Pickard-Cambridge, *The Attic Theatre*, Appendix B.
[4] M 855.

city.[1] A finely preserved text from Lindus on Rhodes,
the "temple chronicle of Athena Lindia," gives us an
excellent idea of the nature of Greek official histories.[2]
Compiled in 99 B.C. from the paper records of magistrates and priests, the inscriptions on ex-votos and the
unofficial local chronicles, it is in substance a list of
notable dedications, with an appendix on the ἐπιφάνειαι
of the goddess. The offerings were mostly credited to
legendary characters, e.g., Cadmus, Minos, Heracles,
Menelaus, and Helen, but historical persons also contributed—Phalaris, Amasis, Alexander, Pyrrhus, and a
Persian nobleman, probably Darius' admiral Datis. Of
the "epiphanies" one took place during an attack by
Datis (494 B.C.?), another at the famous siege by Demetrius.

At the Asclepieum of Epidaurus an official catalogue
of miraculous cures was drawn up, each case being
under a separate rubric. Two long inscriptions preserve
a large assortment of case-records which are of considerable value for the history of Greek medicine.[3]

From Delos we have a document of ninety-four lines
which sets forth in exuberant language how the cult of
Sarapis was introduced into Delos and established with
the help of a timely miracle in the teeth of official
chicanery.[4]

An invaluable source of information, had we but
more of them, would be found in the ἐφημερίδες or
ὑπομνηματισμοί, i.e., court journals, of Alexander and
his successors. One considerable piece from Alexander's own gazette as drawn up by his secretaries

---

[1] O.G.I. 264.
[2] C. Blinkenberg, Die lindische Tempelchronik (Bonn, 1915).
[3] DS 1168-9; Ἐφ. Ἀρχ. 1918-19, p. 157.   [4] I.G. XI, 4, 1299.

Eumenes and Diodotus has been quoted by historians of Alexander.[1] This extract contains a record of the king's transactions in the last week of his reign, and it finds room to mention the continuous potations which hastened on his death.

(5) OFFICIAL DEDICATIONS.—Of these memorials many have survived, mostly on the bases of statues. The chief find spots are Delphi and Olympia, and the largest group of memorials relates to military successes. The following are among the war winners.

Sixth century.—The Athenians (victory over Thebes and Chalcis, *c.* 506 B.C.).[2]

Fifth century.—The Athenians (at Marathon)[3]; the Greek confederates of 480–79 B.C.[4]; Gelo and Hiero;[5] Brasidas and the Acanthians[6]; Lysander and his vice-admirals.[7]

Fourth century.— Conon and Timotheus[8]; the Arcadians and Argives (*c.* 370 B.C.)[9]; the Phocians (ἀπὸ Θεσσάλων)[10]; the Amphictyones (ἀπὸ Φωκέων)[11]; the Rhodians (after the great siege).[12]

Third century.— Pyrrhus (ἀπὸ 'Ρωμαίων)[13]; Antigonus Doson (after Sellasia)[14]; the Pergamene kings (thirty-eight dedications in memory of their Gallic and other wars)[15]; Ptolemy III (after his grand tour through

---

[1] Arrian, *Anabasis* VII, 25; Plutarch, *Alexander*, Ch. 76.
[2] H—H 12. [3] H—H 13; DS 23.
[4] H—H 19; DS 31. This list was engraved on the famous bronze tripods at Delphi.
[5] H—H 16, 22; DS 33-5. [6] DS 79. [7] *F.D.* III, 1, 51-69.
[8] R—G 224. [9] DS 160-1. [10] DS 202-3.
[11] DS 223. [12] DS 441. [13] DS 392.
[14] DS 518. For other dedications at Delos, made in rivalry by the Ptolemies and the Antigonids, see W. Tarn, *J.H.S.* 1909, p. 268 ff.
[15] *Pergamon* 21-39, 51-69.

the Syrian kingdom, of which he gives a detailed account in his dedicatory inscription).[1]

Second century. P. Cornelius Scipio (*c.* 189 B.C.)[2]; Æmilius Paullus[3]; L. Mummius.[4]

The dedications for other than military purposes were mostly by kings and tyrants. Among the rulers who have thus, as it were, left us their visiting cards, we may mention Crœsus (at Ephesus),[5] the Pisistratids (at Athens[6] and at Mt. Ptoius in Bœotia[7]); the exiled Spartan king Pausanias (on a statue of his late son, Agesipolis)[8]; and several Ptolemies who broadcasted their memorials over Greece by way of propaganda.[9]

The legend Κυψελίδαι ἀνέθεν ἐξ Ἡρακλείας, on a gold cup found at Olympia, is, as we have seen,[10] under suspicion of being a forgery. Another inscription which is of doubtful historical value is the dedication under the famous bronze statue of a charioteer at Delphi. The text is so uncertain that the donor has variously been identified with Polyzelus of Syracuse, Anaxilas and Arcesilas.[11]

(6) MISCELLANEOUS OFFICIAL DOCUMENTS.—We may conclude this chapter with an allusion to the bronze tickets of dicasts at Athens, which proved that the holder was qualified to sit on a jury,[12] and to a considerable collection of hymns and liturgies for use at the

---

[1] H 173.
[2] *Klio*, 1923, p. 153-4, no. 138.
[3] DS 652*a* (in Latin).   [4] M 1090.
[5] H—H 5; DS 6.
[6] Thuc. VI, 54; H—H 10; M 1019.   [7] *B.C.H.* 1920, p. 238.
[8] *I.G.* V, 1, p. xxi, no. 1565.
[9] *O.G.I.* 15-35.
[10] P. 3.
[11] For recent interpretations of this text, see F. Poulsen, *Delphi*, pp. 222-5.
[12] H—H 151; R—G 395-400.

principal religious festivals.[1] The most noteworthy of these latter documents are two hymns sung by Attic choirs at the Delphic festival of the Pythais (138 and 128 B.C.), over which the melody is inscribed in musical notation. The score has been transcribed by modern scholars to our stave notation and is now perhaps our best means of appreciating Greek music.[2]

[1] See especially J. U. Powell, *Analecta Alexandrina.*
[2] Th. Reinach, in *FD* III, pt. 2, pp. 147-169; D. B. Monro, *Modes of Greek Music*, p. 134.

CHAPTER VI

JUDICIAL RECORDS

Extraordinary Procedure.—In Greek city-states jurisdiction was not entirely reserved to the regular tribunals. Cases of a political character were not infrequently appropriated by the Boule or Ecclesia and there settled by an expeditious procedure. The most rough-and-ready of such trials was by ostracism. Records of these judgments survive in potsherds that served as voting-tickets for the Athenian ecclesiasts. The earliest ostracisms are commemorated on stray pieces bearing the names of Megacles, Xanthippus, and Themistocles.[1] Another contest, probably that of 443 B.C., is illustrated by a recently discovered dump of sherds which had been tipped into the town moat.[2] The loser in the trial of 443 B.C., Thucydides, son of Melesias, is inscribed on eleven pieces, a certain Cleippides on twenty-four, Andocides and others on one.

The sentences inflicted by Greek Ecclesiæ for serious political offences, such as treason, were usually published on special στῆλαι,[3] of which several specimens have been preserved. On a fifth-century text from

---

[1] H—H 14.
[2] *A.M.* 1915, p. 1 ff., with corrections in do., 1922, p. 1 ff.
[3] *E.g.*, the stone at Athens which proclaimed the outlawry of the Pisistratids. (Thuc. VI, 55.)

Miletus we read a sentence of outlawry upon some revolutionary leaders, probably oligarchs who had belied Athenian trustfulness.[1] The famous trial of Antiphon in 411 B.C. is commemorated by two surviving texts, the former of which contains instructions for the commitment of Antiphon and others to trial, while the latter records the sentence passed upon them.[2] A conspiracy against Mausolus is brought to our notice in an inscription of Mylasa which records judgment upon the guilty parties,[3] and an episode of the Sacred War is illustrated by a bronze tablet at Delphi containing a list of families proscribed in 353 B.C. at the instance of Onomarchus.[4] In a decree of Eresus which records sentences passed on two ex-tyrants we obtain a lurid picture of the brutalities perpetrated by some of the ruffians who enlisted under Alexander, but, it is fair to add, were repudiated by him and his successors.[5] On a text from Dyme we have a case of false coining for which the death penalty was inflicted. The culprits had concealed their names under aliases.[6]

The judicial powers of Greek βουλαί are illustrated by two inscriptions, from Ceos (fifth century), and Epidaurus (third century), in both of which the Council confirms a previous sentence and raises the fine by half.[7]

Another kind of special tribunal which played an important part in Greece was the court of arbitration set up to pronounce upon inter-state disputes. The success which usually attended the work of such courts

---

[1] DS 58. For the occasion, cf. [Xenophon], Ἀθηναίων Πολιτεία III, 11.
[2] [Plutarch], Vitæ X Oratorum, p. 833 E—F.
[3] H—H 133 ; DS 167. [4] DS 177.
[5] H—H 157; M 358. [6] M 1339.
[7] M 1341, 1336.

has already been noticed in our review of the votes of thanks passed in honour of the arbitrators (Ch. III, pp. 32-3). Of their decisions, which were usually published on stone copies, numerous examples survive, and from these the character of the disputes and the technique of the arbitral procedure is chiefly made known to us.[1] Decidedly the commonest kind of case to come to court was a quarrel about frontiers. A few leading examples may here be given. (i) Twenty-five judges drawn from five Ionian cities and empanelled by the Persian satrap Struses apportion the lower Mæander valley between Miletus and Myus (c. 390 B.C.).[2] (ii) The Ecclesia of Argos, by the mandate of the Hellenic League of 338 B.C., settles a dispute between Melos and Cimolos concerning some adjacent islets.[3] (iii) King Lysimachus communicates at length with the Samians concerning the past history of a border strip over which they and the Prienians had wrangled since the time of the sage Bias.[4] (iv) One hundred and fifty-one Megarians appointed by the Achæan League revise the boundaries between Corinth and Epidaurus; the Corinthians contest the award, whereupon an inner court of thirty-one Megarians revisits the debatable land and makes a final settlement (c. 240 B.C.).[5] (v) The Roman prætor Q. Calpurnius refers a long-standing dispute between Sparta and Messene to a Milesian court, which con-

---

[1] On this subject see A. Raeder, *L'arbitrage international chez les Hellènes* (eighty-one cases, of which fifty-three are derived from inscriptions), and especially M. N. Tod, *International Arbitration amongst the Greeks*, who passes eighty-two epigraphic texts under review.
[2] DS 134; Tod 70.
[3] H—H 150; Tod 47.   [4] H 152; Tod 61.
[5] DS 471; *I.J.G.* I. 16; Tod 15. For a similar case, in which judges from eleven towns of the Achæan League arbitrated between Epidaurus and Arsinoe-Methone, see Ἐφ. Ἀρχ. 1918-19, p. 151 ff.

firms the Messenian claim by 584 votes to 16 (*c.* 145 B.C.).[1]

A complex money transaction between the towns of Calymna and some money-lenders of Cos is recounted in a long document in which minute rules are also laid down for the court at Cnidus (second century).[2] But the most exacting case of all was a fifth-century dispute which Cnossus and Tylissus in Crete referred to Argos. The award, which embraced agrarian, commercial, and religious issues, runs into fourteen clauses.[3]

(2) PROCEDURE IN ORDINARY COURTS.—The records of the ordinary Greek tribunals were not as a rule made out in duplicate. Very few specimens have been preserved on stone, and not many more have survived in the texts of the Attic orators[4]; but a large number of juristic papyri has been discovered in Egypt.

(*a*) *Writs.*—In addition to some stray specimens in the speeches of the Attic orators,[5] we possess the texts of two writs of special historical importance. One of these was taken out by Thessalus the son of Cimon against Alcibiades,[6] the other was issued by Anytus and others against Socrates. The latter runs as follows: "Socrates does wrong in that he does not worship the gods whom the city worships but introduces other evil powers; and he does wrong in that he corrupts young men. Penalty proposed: death."[7]

[1] H 200; DS 683; Tod 1.
[2] DS 953; *I.J.G.* I. 10; Tod, 75.   [3] DS 56; Tod, 51.
[4] The processual documents quoted in Demosthenes, *De Corona* are palpably fictitious; those of the speech *In Midiam* and of Lycurgus' suit *In Leocratem* are deeply suspect.
[5] *E.g.*, Dem. 37 § 22.   [6] Plutarch, *Alcibiades*, Ch. 22.
[7] Diogenes Lærtius, *Life of Socrates* II, 5, 40. This text comes from a late and uncritical author, but it is correctly formulated, and the document which it reproduces is said to have remained on view at the Athenian Record Office.

(*b*) *Petitions.*—In Egypt a common method of initiating a suit was by petition. The plea was usually addressed to the king himself, but was in most cases lodged with the *strategus* (county governor), who appears to have had much work thrust upon him owing to the dilatoriness or worse of the lower officials. The petitions are mostly by humble people, who apply for restitution of property,[1] for protection against harsh creditors,[2] for security against unlawful arrest,[3] for delivery from protracted detention.[4] In one poignant case a beggar-girl complains of robbery[5]; in another a bather claims damages in respect of a scalding by a clumsy attendant[6]; in a third the parent of a susceptible youth applies for the annulment of a bond written under the glad eyes of a professional beauty.[7] Another full docket of actions was provided by military allotment-holders who suffered from acquisitive neighbours[8] or were the victims of assaults.[9] Two famous suits are on record in which pertinacious claimants repeated their demands to the point of universal exhaustion. In one instance a pair of twin orphan sisters who had found billets as temple attendants but did not receive their stipulated rations of bread and oil dinned their grievance into the king's capacious ears, undeterred by official snubs.[10] In the second of these "Jarndyce *v.* Jarndyce" suits an ex-officer named Hermias waged a

[1] *E.g., P. Lille* II. 4 (theft of pigs); II. 13 (a dishonest pawnbroker).
[2] *P. Reinach*, 18.   [3] *P. Petr.* II, 10 (2); *P. Tebt.* I, 43.
[4] *P. Petr.* III, 36; *P. Lille* I, 7; *PSI.* 347. (10-12 months in duress on starvation diet.)
[5] *P. Lond.* I, 24.
[6] *P. Lille* II, 33.   [7] *P. Lille* II, 14.
[8] *P. Lille* II, 1.
[9] *P. Lille* II. *passim.* The assailants often were native Egyptians.
[10] U. Wilcken, *Urkunden der Ptolemäerzeit* II, 17-56; *P. Lond.* I, p. 1 ff.

ten years' war about the possession of an estate to which his claim was apparently quite untenable.[1]

(c) *Judgments.*—The principal specimens from Greece are sentences passed at the great athletic festivals upon offenders against the rules of the course, which it was usual to exhibit on durable copies. A bronze tablet from Olympia records a penalty of thirty Æginetan minæ imposed by the Hellanodicæ for violence against the θεωροί or official representatives of a city (sixth or fifth century).[2] Stone slabs from the Asclepieum at Epidaurus bear record of fines levied upon a sprinter for foul play and upon a troupe of actors for scratching an event.[3]

From Egypt we have entire lists of petty fines inflicted for breaches of the peace, thefts of donkeys, etc.; the amounts range from one to eighty drachmas.[4] In one remarkable case a village Hampden is punished for the crime of defending a debtor in a revenue suit[5]; in another a number of grave-diggers is sentenced for carrying off dead bodies.[6] The humaner side of Ptolemaic jurisdiction is shown up in an extensive class of documents recording renunciations or abatements of a suitor's claim as the result of friendly negotiations, such as the judges of the lower courts were usually instructed to conduct before instituting a formal trial.[7]

(d) *Executions.*—These are illustrated by a lengthy papyrus containing a judge's instruction to a bailiff and setting out the circumstances of a quite straightforward case with superfluous detail.[8]

[1] A. Peyron, *Papyri Græci et Latini* (Turin), nos. 1-4. J. P. Mahaffy, *The Empire of the Ptolemies,* p. 401. [2] *Olymp.* 13.
[3] M 1337-8. [4] *P. Hibeh* I, 111. [5] *P. Amherst* II, 33. [6] *P. Rylands* II, 65.
[7] A good example of such συγχωρήσεις is afforded by *P. Hibeh* I, 96.
[8] P. M. Meyer, *Juristiche Papyri,* no. 79.

CHAPTER VII

STATE DESPATCHES.—The territorial dimensions of the city-state were small enough to allow of its business being transacted by word of mouth or by public poster. A letter service was therefore only required for dealings with foreign powers or generals in the field. Of this kind of despatch very few specimens have been preserved.

The long explanatory message in which Nicias broke the news about the impending disaster at Syracuse has been reproduced in substance by Thucydides.[1] In Xenophon we read the actual words in which Mindarus' vice-admiral blurted out the story of Cyzicus: "ships all gone; Mindarus missing; men starving; we don't know what to do."[2] Of the foreign correspondence of Athens in the fourth century we possess a letter by Philip of Macedon remonstrating with the Athenians for their unfriendly attitude.[3] This missive in its present form is a composition by the rhetorician Anaximenes, but it probably gives the substance of Philip's actual despatch.[4]

The letters which Pausanias and Themistocles were

[1] Thuc. VII. 11-15.
[2] *Hellenica* I, 1, 23. This despatch owes its survival to the Athenians having intercepted and published it.
[3] [Dem.] 11.
[4] See P. Wendland, *Anaximenes von Lampsakos.*

72

alleged to have addressed to the kings of Persia[1] are, to say the least, under suspicion, for it is difficult to see how their contents could become public. The despatch of Agesilaus announcing the conquest of "most of Asia" and his return home at the ephors' behest may be safely set down as a pious fraud.[2] On the other hand, the reply of Xerxes to Pausanias[3] may perfectly well be genuine, and there is no good reason for suspecting the characteristic despatch of Darius in which the king reprimanded a Persian official for trespassing upon Greek temple land at Magnesia.[4]

In the Hellenistic age the letter-patent ($\delta\iota\acute{a}\gamma\rho\alpha\mu\mu\alpha$) became an important means of communication between sovereigns and subjects. A considerable number of these messages was engraved on stone slabs (in some cases by royal order), and has thus survived.

Of the despatches of Alexander we possess a letter to the Chians, commanding them to furnish a fleet and submit a draft of a new constitution (333–2 B.C.),[5] and the famous circular which caused such a stir at the Olympic games of 324 B.C., to the effect that all exiles from Greek states were to be received home.[6] Thus the king is proved by his own writ to have violated the autonomy of his Greek allies. The various other letters of Alexander which are reproduced by Greek authors, and especially his correspondence with his mother, are almost certainly forgeries.[7]

---

[1] Thuc. I, 128, 137.
[2] Plut., *Apophthegmata Laconica, Agesilaus*, no. 41.
[3] Thuc. I, 129.   [4] H—H 20; DS 22.
[5] H—H 158; DS 283.   [6] Diodorus XVIII, 8.
[7] See especially J. Kaerst in *Philologus*, 1892, p. 601 ff. The defence of these letters by E. Pridik, *De Alexandri Magni epistularum commercio* (Dorpat, 1893) hardly meets Kaerst's criticisms. (But see H. Berve, *Das Alexanderreich* p. 44, n. 2, for the opposite view.)

In contrast with Alexander's missives the ably written proclamation of Polyperchon (318 B.C.) re-affirms the original constitution of the Hellenic League against the encroachments of Alexander and Antipater.[1] Similarly Antigonus I at least preserves the appearance of dealing with allies rather than subjects. In a long rescript to the towns of Lebedus and Teos in which he regulates the συνοικισμός of these places with minute detail, he couches his commands in the form of advice (οἰόμεθα δεῖν . . .), and he makes a substantial if reluctant concession to the cities by allowing them to divert part of their tribute into a corn-purchase fund (c. 305 B.C.).[2] In a letter to the town of Scepsis the same ruler garrulously protests his fair intentions and expatiates on the good news that he has just concluded peace with his fellow Diadochi (311 B.C.).[3]

Of the Seleucid correspondence the most interesting piece is the "Laodice inscription" from Didyma.[4] This document contains a series of instructions passed down from Antiochus II of Syria to his satrap at Sardes, and from the satrap to his secretariat, concerning the sale of a large territory, together with its serf population, to the ex-queen Laodice, and the setting up of five copies of the transfer deed. In another despatch Seleucus II announces to the Milesians an act of generosity on his part to the temple at Didyma and appends a list of his gifts.[5]

A somewhat more masterful attitude is revealed in a missive from Eumenes I to Pergamum, commanding

---

[1] Diod. XVIII, 56.   [2] H 149; DS 344.   [3] O.G.I. 5.
[4] O.G.I. 225; Th. Wiegand in *Abh. Berl. Ak.* 1908, Anhang, p. 35; Wilhelm, *Neue Beiträge* III, p. 40.
[5] H 175; M 3

the Ecclesia of that city to pay public honours to the strategi whom he had imposed upon it.[1] On the other hand Attalus II in a series of letters to a high priest of Cybele tamely apologises for his failure to put down some Gallic marauders, explaining that in his Privy Council he had been warned not to offend the Romans by too great a display of activity.[2]

Two letters from Philip V of Macedon to Larissa show up this king in his sober mood. He politely but insistently advises the Larissæans to be liberal with their franchise and holds up before them the shining example of the Romans, who even gave office to ex-slaves and by virtue of their generosity in bestowing citizenship had been able to found seventy [sic] colonies.[3]

Most of the earlier Ptolemies have left us specimens of their correspondence. The most valuable of these is a communiqué of Ptolemy III concerning his campaign in Syria, cast in the form of a letter to his queen. In this despatch he gives out that on arriving at Seleucia he found his sister Berenice still alive, but this may have been an official fiction with a view to strengthening his case against Seleucus II.[4] Scarcely inferior in interest is a proclamation of 264 lines by Ptolemy VIII, announcing a general remission of fiscal debts and reproving his officials for vexatious billetings and the use of false measures.[5] From Ptolemy I we have a sharp letter to a quartermaster calling upon him to check unruly be-

---

[1] *O.G.I.* 267.
[2] M 45. *Cf.* the advice given by Callicrates to the Achæan League (Polyb. 33, 15, 7).
[3] M 41.
[4] *Chrest* I, 1; Wilamowitz-Moellendorff, *Hermes*, 1914, p. 447 ff.
[5] *P. Tebt.* I, 5.

haviour by the troops,[1] and from Ptolemy V a similar note to a district magistrate reprimanding him for wrongful ar.ests.[2]

Several letters written by Roman magistrates to Greek states have been preserved. In 190 B.C. Lucius Scipio, in consultation with his famous brother, wrote to Heraclea-on-Latmus conveying a grant of freedom on his own authority.[3] A similar favour, by order of the Senate, was announced to Delphi by a despatch from the praetor Postumius in 189 B.C.[4] Another despatch, from an unknown official of 171 B.C., relates to the Delphic Amphictyony the catalogue of king Perseus' public offences.[5]

(2) ROUTINE CORRESPONDENCE.—In Egypt, where the "culte de la paperasse" had taken root in Pharaonic times and flourished more than ever in the Ptolemaic era, whole bundles of official correspondence have come to light. Only in rare cases do these letters come from the hand of a higher magistrate, such as Ptolemy II's finance minister Apollonius, and his chief commissioner of works, Cleon; most of them illustrate the routine work of the lower officials and their dealings with the general public. The endless variety of these documents makes selection difficult, but the following examples may serve to show their general character.

(a) *Superior officials to subordinates.*—The correspondence of the minister Apollonius with his bailiff Zeno includes a whole dossier of instructions relating to the

---

[1] *Dikaiomata* I, p. 98.
[2] F. Preisigke, *Sammelbuch griechischer Urkunden aus Aegypten,* no. 5675.
[3] DS 618; De Sanctis, *Rivista di Filologia,* 1924, p. 29 ff. (where the authorship of L. Scipio is proved).
[4] DS 612. For the whole dossier of Roman letters to Delphi at this period, see *Klio,* 1923, pp. 119-135.
[5] DS 643

development of a latifundium with which Apollonius was charged as with a λειτουργία or public service. Like a true Greek, Apollonius was chiefly interested in improvements by plantation, hence his repeated orders to stock his park-land with olive-shoots, pear-shoots, apple-trees, laurels, and firs.[1] But he also experimented by royal command with a catch crop on the tillage land to follow the usual April harvest.[2]

In other papyrus collections we read orders from a strategus (district magistrate) to his superintendent of granaries to distribute seed-corn after a lean year,[3] to his surveyor to inspect and measure the allotment-land of the reservist troops,[4] to his collector to call in estates on the reservists' demise or departure.[5] The government's control over trade is exemplified by warrants for the arrest of oil retailers who had exceeded the government price,[6] and of a woman who had sold oil without a licence.[7] Other instances of official rigour will be found in a reprimand, 200 lines long, addressed to a treasury official for imposing illicit taxes and task-work[8]; in a friendly hint from a colleague to Zeno to send in his accounts to Apollonius and explain the absence of certain seven talents from his chief's strong-box[9]; in an inquiry made by Apollonius of Zeno's predecessor why his report is not to hand, and an answer to Apollonius giving a hundred good reasons for the delay.[10]

The awe which ordinary officials felt for important

---

[1] *A.S.A.* XVIII, no. 21 (p. 243); XXIV, nos. 94-5 (p. 25-7), 100 (pp. 31-2).
[2] *Ibid.* XIX, no. 27 (p. 21).   [3] *P. Lille*, I, 5, II, 39-51.
[4] *P. Freiburg*, No. 2. The inspection was apparently intended to make sure that the native sub-tenants paid their rent.
[5] *P. Lille*, I, 14; *Hibeh*, 81.   [6] *P. Lille*, I, 3, l. 55.
[7] *P. Hibeh*, 59.   [8] *P. Petr.* III, p. 15 ff.
[9] *P.S.I.* IV, 411. *Cf. P. Tebt.* I, 17 ("inspectors coming").
[10] *P.S.I.* V, 502.

personages is revealed in a letter of advice from a strategus to a subordinate to make the way smooth for a friend of Apollonius on his travels,[1] and a more specific injunction to provide for the journey of a grandee "50 geese, 200 birds, 100 doves, 5 saddle and 40 luggage asses."[2] In another letter, which must have been more welcome to its recipients, a party of elephant hunters in the far south is notified that an overdue relief ship is about to reach them.[3] Lastly, we may note a recurrent formula in the instructions sent by strategi to the lower courts: "if possible, effect a reconciliation between the parties."[4]

(b) *Subordinates to their chiefs.*—These for the most part are requests for information or assistance. Bailiffs send up for policemen to watch over harvest or vintage,[5] a necessary precaution, for one of them had to report a theft of full thirty-thousand vine stakes.[6] One unfortunate under-bailiff implores Zeno to sell an estate because he had had enough of his labourers' drunken insolence (παροινία).[7] An official of the works department suggests to his chief an imposition of extra corvée for the completion of a canal and the remission of salt duty by way of compensation.[8] A financial official reports a case of illicit land enclosure and the application of "forcible persuasion" (πειθανάγκη) to the offender.[9] Zeno's salesman renders an account of a transaction in wheat and reckons up his cash balance.[10] An agent of

---

[1] *P.S.I.* V, 520. *Cf. A.S.A.* XXIV, no. 92 (p. 31-2).
[2] *P. Grenfell* II, 13b. Another grandee was content with five stuffed geese (*P. Heidelberg*, no. 2).
[3] *P. Petr.* II, 40.   [4] *E.g. Chrest.* II, 10-11; Lille II, *passim.*
[5] *P.S.I.* IV, 345; V. 490.   [6] *P.S.I.* IV, 393.   [7] *Ibid.* 352.
[8] *P. Petr.* II, 4, no. 11.   [9] *P. Amherst,* 31.
[10] *P. Michigan,* 245 (published in *Aegyptus* II, p. 285).

Apollonius at the Alexandrian mint inquires on what terms he is to accept used coins and gold plate for conversion into specie.[1] A ship's captain indents for a tamarisk stump to repair his craft.[2] Lastly, a clerk advises Zeno that he has purchased ten rolls of papyrus for the office.[3] To judge by what remains of Zeno's correspondence, this supply did not last long.

(c) *Private persons to officials.*—In addition to the legal petitions which we have already noticed (Ch. VI, p. 70), we possess various other specimens of addresses from the king's subjects to his administrators. As might be expected, many of these are protests against oppressive tax-gatherers[4] or unfair billetings.[5] Herdsmen complain about the seizure of their geese,[6] temple assistants cry out against a harvesting fatigue and claim that their duties begin and end with feeding the cats[7]; quarrymen lay an indictment against their ganger, who submits a rejoinder[8]; a pumpkin-seller pleads that he cannot pay his trade licence because the lentil-roasters are taking away his custom.[9] Letters recommending a young aspirant to a job are not unknown; others contain offers by peasants to take up leases,[10] by contractors to build dykes,[11] by craftsmen to work up government cloth.[12] A bird fancier reports to Zeno the despatch of some choice specimens, describing each fowl's plumage[13]; a group of weavers suggest to him an advance in piece rates or the substitution of payment by time[14]; a slave girl complains that she is worn out with carrying timber, but cozeningly protests that she won't run away "like the rest,"

[1] *A.S.A.* XVIII, no. 5 (167–71).   [2] *P.S.I.* IV, 382
[3] *Ibid.* V, 519.   [4] *Ibid.* IV, 383-4.   [5] *P. Petr.* III, 20.
[6] *Ibid.* II, 10 (1).   [7] *P.S.I.* IV, 440.   [8] *P. Petr.* II, 4, nos. 1-2.
[9] *P.S.I.* IV, 402.   [10] *P. Eleph.* 19-25.   [11] *P.S.I.* V, 488.
[12] *Ibid.* IV, 341.   [13] *Ibid.* VI, 569.   [14] *Ibid.* VI, 599.

because "I know your ways, how you hate meanness in folks" (ὅτι μισοπόνηρος εἶ).[1]

Miscellaneous details.—In concluding this survey of official documents, we would point out that studied *collectively* these throw much light on a mass of points of detail such as the procedure of public bodies, the sanctions by which decrees were enforced, the titles and functions of the various executive officials, the degree of fusion between Greeks and non-Greeks in foreign lands like Egypt and Scythia, the personalities of the leading politicians in Athens and other states.[2] Of the numerous notable facts which modern scholars have gleaned by this process it may suffice to mention one. By a close study of Attic inscriptions of the fourth century the Finnish scholar Sundwall has proved that the administration of Athens at that period was largely in the hands of the well-to-do, and that the φυγαρχία which Plato noticed had not set in at any rate in his native town.[3]

APPENDIX. *Records in oriental languages.*—Documentary evidence for Greek History consists almost wholly of texts written by Greeks, or at any rate in Greek. But an occasional light is thrown on Greek events by records in Oriental tongues. From the annals of the Assyrian kings we learn that in 715 B.C. Sargon expelled an "Ionian" tyrant from Ashdod, and that in 698 Sanherib defeated some more "Ionians," presumably pirates, in Cilicia.[4] In 709 Sargon received gifts

---

[1] *Ibid.* VI, 667.

[2] See especially W. Larfeld, *Griechische Epigraphik* and *Handbuch der griechischen Epigraphik*, and S. Reinach, *Traité d'épigraphie grecque.*

[3] *Klio Beiheft*, IV.

[4] L. King, *Cuneiform Inscriptions of Western Asia*, I, pl. 36, l. 21; *J.H.S.* 1910, p. 327, 331. A.T. Olmstead, in *Anatolian Studies dedicated to Sir W.M. Ramsay*, pp. 289-90.

(perhaps in hope of trade concessions) from seven kings of Cyprus who bore Greek names,[1] and Esarhaddon was similarly courted by ten rulers of Cyprus.[2] On the other hand Asshurbanipal's account of overtures from Gyges of Lydia is suspect and should not be used to correct Herodotus' story.[3] The great Persian rock inscription is chiefly of negative value, in that among the many rebellions against Darius not a single Greek movement finds a mention. The paragraph relating to Darius' expedition to Scythia unfortunately throws very little light on this venture.[4] At Babylon astronomical calendars have been discovered which serve to elucidate the chronology of the Seleucid kings. These also disclose the unexpected fact that in 302 B.C. Antigonus I drove Seleucus out of Babylon.[5]

Demotic papyri from Egypt contain numerous records of suits in native courts to which Greeks were parties. Thus the famous "Hermias case" (pp. 70-1) went before an Egyptian tribunal in one stage of its long career, and is therefore commemorated in demotic records.[6] In other demotic documents Greeks or persons with Greek names appear as parties to commercial and matrimonial contracts.[7] But on the whole this class of papyrus has more value for the lawyer than for the historian.

[1] R. W. Rogers, *History of Babylon and Assyria*, II, p. 340.
[2] A. T. Olmstead, *History of Assyria*, p. 369.
[3] A. T. Olmstead, *Anatolian Studies*, pp. 295-6.
[4] L. King, *The Inscription of Darius the Great at Behistun*, § 74.
[5] F. Kugler, *Von Moses bis Paulus*, Ch. VI, with the criticisms of W. Tarn in the *Classical Review*, 1926, pp. 13-15; Ed. Meyer, *Forschungen zur alten Geschichte*, II, p. 453 ff. *Cf.* also S. Smith. *Babylonian Historical Texts, ch.* 5 (a chronicle of 321-312 B.C.).
[6] E. Revillout, *Le Procès d'Hermias d'après les papyrus démotiques.*
[7] Th. Reinach and W. Spiegelberg, *Papyrus grecs et démotiques*; W. Spiegelberg, *Die demotischen Papyri Hauswaldt*, Vol. II.

CHAPTER VIII

PRIVATE DOCUMENTS

THE Greeks were slower to perceive the advantages of keeping records in their private than in their public affairs, and it was not until the Hellenistic age that they amassed private archives or set up offices for the storing of these, after the fashion of the Egyptians and Babylonians. But from the time of Alexander private documents form an appreciable supplement to the public records. The following selection may serve for example.

(1) *Acts of betrothal.*—A running list of these stands on a third-century stone from Myconos, where a public registrar took charge of their publication. As usual in Greek law, the bride was not a party to the covenant, but her position was secured by a dowry, for due payment of which her father sometimes mortgaged a property.[1]

(2) *Marriage contracts.*—Surviving specimens on Egyptian papyri form a fairly numerous and uniform class. Of these a compact dated 311-10 B.C. may be taken as a type. The husband may divorce the wife and retain her dowry if he can prove infidelity on her part to three witnesses; but if misconduct is proved against him he must return the dowry and pay a fine in addi-

[1] DS 1215; *I.J.G.* I, 6. For an Attic mortgage as cover for a dowry; *Cf.* M 1368.

tion. He is also bound to find the wife in all proper appurtenances (ὅσα προσήκει).[1] This agreement closely follows the marriage deeds described by the Attic orators.

(3) *Manumissions.*—Of the procedures recognised by Greek law for the emancipation of slaves, the simplest was to make a declaration before a magistrate and pay a registration fee. The surviving records of this class are all of late date. A good specimen is preserved on a stone from Melitæa containing a list of persons who had paid the statutory sum of fifteen staters for attestation.[2] Another and perhaps commoner method was to dedicate the slave *pro forma* to a god, who guaranteed the freedman's new status against all claimants and waived his own rights to service. Inscriptions attesting such fictitious consecrations have been discovered at several Greek temple-sites, but by far the largest collection comes from Delphi.[3] The Delphic records are all cast in similar form, but the rates of ransom vary greatly, and there is considerable diversity in the services which the manumittor exacted during his lifetime from his former slave. From Egypt we have deeds in which payment of τροφεῖα (a compensation to the former owner?) is attested, and a special clause is inserted to debar any further claims by the manumittor.[4]

(4) *Wills.*—Of this class we possess some early examples which carry curtness to the point of obscurity

---

[1] *P. Eleph.* 1 (G. Milligan, *Selections from the Greek Papyri*, No. 1). *Cf.* a second-century papyrus (J. Nicole, *Les papyrus de Genève*, no. 21, pp. 30–33), in which the wife is expressly permitted to divorce.

[2] *I.G.* IX, 2, 206. For other examples, *cf.* G. Rensch, *De Manumissionum. Titulis apud Thessalos.*

[3] *I.J.G.* II. 30; M 1388-1426; A. Calderini, *La manomissione e le condizione dei liberti in Grecia.* Cf. also DS 1204-12.

[4] *P. Eleph.* 3-4.

and stand in contrast with the long-winded documents
of the later age. On a bronze tablet of *c.* 500 B.C. from
Petelia in S. Italy we read the following simple declaration: "Saotis giveth to Sicania the houses and all else."[1]
Some testaments of the Hellenistic period, in which
wealthy donors set up trusts, are as circumstantial as
similar modern deeds: in founding a commemorative
cult a third-century lady required 284 lines to express
her intentions.[2] But the most remarkable feature about
these Hellenistic endowments is their number: at Delos
no less than twenty-four foundations have been counted
in the century after Alexander.[3] A large collection of
soldiers' wills has survived on papyri. These, of course,
are of military brevity, but since the men wore no
identity discs personal descriptions of them, like those
on our passports, had to be inserted.[4]

(5) *Epitaphs.*—The Greeks did most of their talking
while they lived, and not until the period of Roman
domination did they acquire the habit of posthumous
garrulity. Even then they took to poetry rather than to
historical narrative.[5] Greek tombstones therefore are
less informative than Roman ones. The most important
of the Greek epitaphs are the semi-public ones which
the poet Simonides composed in honour of men who
fell in the Persian Wars.[6] These both confirm and correct the history of Herodotus. The verses in memory
of Marathon and the Eurymedon reflect the Athenian

[1] M 1346.
[2] M 1001; *I.J.G.* II, 24. *Cf.* DS 1106 (a Coan testament).
[3] E. Ziebarth, *Hermes*, 1917, p. 425 ff. On the whole subject *cf.* B. Laum, *Stiftungen in der griechischen und römischen Antike.*
[4] *P. Petr.* III, 1-19.
[5] *Cf.* the numerous specimens in G. Kaibel, *Epigrammata Graeca.*
[6] Some of these poems may not be by Simonides' own hand; but in this case his imitators caught the spirit of the times as truly as Simonides himself.

belief that these were epoch-making victories.[1] The famous lines, "ὦ ξεῖν’, ἀγγέλλειν", etc., similarly reproduces the Spartan version of Leonidas’ death to which Herodotus too has given expression, that Spartans always died at their posts[2]; and in another couplet we obtain what was perhaps the official estimate of the forces engaged at Thermopylæ, "4,000 Peloponnesians *versus* 300,000 Persians."[3] Of the minor combatants the Locrians[4] and Megarians[5] receive due mention, and the Corinthians, together with their admiral, Adeimantus are vindicated against the libels which Herodotus transmitted about them.[6] The only other epitaph that requires mention commemorates the bravery of a Bœotian knight who rode in eighteen charges during an action against Antigonus Gonatas (292 B.C.).[7]

(6) *Club records.*—In accordance with the fact that Greek clubs, other than purely religious associations, were mushroom growths of the Hellenistic age, the documents relating to them are of late date. The records are very numerous, and they provide a mass of information on a subject about which our literary texts are almost reticent.[8] The rules of these societies are illustrated by a νόμος εἰσαγωγῆς from Tenos, prescribing the conditions under which wives and sons of members might come in, and the sacrifices required as entrance fees[9]; and by a long text relating to a society

---

[1] Frs. 93, 109-111 (ed. Bergk.).   [2] Fr. 95.
[3] Fr. 94.   [4] Fr. 100.   [5] Fr. 112.
[6] Frs. 102-3, 105. The actual stone on which fr. 102 was inscribed has been found at Salamis (H—H 18). Only the first two lines of Simonides’ poem are legible here.
[7] B.C.H. 1900, p. 70.
[8] On this subject see E. Ziebarth, *Das griechische Vereinswesen*, and F. Poland, *Geschichte des griechischen Vereinswesens*.
[9] *Revue archéologique*, 1917, p. 54 ff.

of "Iobacchi" at Athens, in which, significantly enough, provision is made for separating members who had fallen to fighting and for ejecting disturbers.[1] Of the many resolutions passed by club members in the form of ψηφίσματα we may select for special mention the decrees of the τεχνῖται περὶ τὸν Διόνυσον or professional actors, who were grouped together in powerful unions with headquarters at Athens, Corinth, Teos, and elsewhere, and had branch establishments all over the Greek world.[2] A list of τεχνῖται, including poets, musicians and makers of "property," is preserved in a decree from Ptolemais in Upper Egypt.[3] Club catalogues with bare lists of names are not uncommon, but require no comment.

(7) *Records relating to religion.* (i) *Club documents.*— These largely consist of ἐπαινέσεις of dutiful priests and priestesses, or of ritual regulations, and conform to the pattern of the state records which we have already examined.[4] Perhaps the most interesting records of this order relate to the introduction of new deities in which the clubs took a large part.[5]

(ii) *Dedications.*[6]—The private offerings at Greek shrines include many gifts by notable personalities. A large and characteristic class consists of dedications by victorious athletes. The list opens with an inscription of *c.* 600 B.C. on a stone at Olympia which weighs 316 lbs. The legend declares that one Bybon hove this

---

[1] DS 1109.
[2] M 1009-18; *Magn.* 89.
[3] M 1017.
[4] For instances of religious laws, *cf.* M 702-735.
[5] For the introduction of the Sarapis cult at Delos *cf.* Ch. V. p. 62. On the whole subject of religious clubs, see P. Foucart, *Les Associations religieuses chez les Grecs.*
[6] On dedications in general, see W. H. D. Rouse, *Greek Votive Offerings.*

Sisyphæan weight over his head with one hand![1] After this, one would expect to find that the statue of the Crotonian Phaÿllus at Delphi (c. 480 B.C.) should mention his reputed jump of fifty-five feet, but in fact it lets the mere name of Phaÿllus speak for itself.[2] An amazing but authentic record of c. 470 B.C. attributes[3] 1,300 victories to the boxer Theogenes of Thasos. Other athletic celebrities whose feats are commemorated by dedications are Cynisca, daughter of king Archidamus,[4] Dorieus of Rhodes, a great pancratiast of the late fifth century,[5] and a Thessalian grandee of the fourth century, named Daochus, who boasted that he defeated all comers and killed one antagonist outright.[6] In addition to the above "internationals," who won their events at the panhellenic πανηγύρεις, many winners of local tourneys have commemorated their exploits. Perhaps the most notable of these was a Spartan athlete of the fifth century named Damonon, who began as a boy runner and ended as a celebrated jockey.[7] Another remarkable dedication was that which "Alcmæonides son of Alcmæon" made at the shrine of Apollo Ptoius to commemorate a victory at the Panathenæa (c. 550-540 B.C.)[8]: this was no doubt a counterblast to the offering of Hipparchus at the same sanctuary (Ch. V, p. 64). To this list of dedications by athletes we may add the offerings of successful χορηγοί at the dramatic or musical festivals at Athens. These include a gift by two rich men who helped Sophocles and Aristophanes to gain prizes.[9]

---

[1] *Olymp.* 717. [2] DS 30. [3] DS 36. [4] *Olymp.* 160.
[5] DS 82. [6] M 1281. [7] *I.G.* V, 1, 213. [8] *B.C.H.* 1920, p. 228.
[9] R—G 180-4; cf. also R—G 217 (the inscription on the monument of Lysicrates).

Among the other private donors we meet with several familiar names. The "Cleobis" and "Bito"[1] of a Delphic inscription are of course the heroes of Herodotus' well-known tale (I, 31). Under the seated statues at Didyma we find the names "Thales"[2] and "Histæus"[3], and at Naucratis a cup dedicated to Aphrodite is inscribed "Herodotus."[4] But it would be rash to assert that these represent the historian and two of his chief characters: indeed, the Thale of the inscription is proved by his father's name (Python) to be different from Herodutus' Thales (son of Hexamyes). It is also difficult to draw any conclusions from the "Sigeum bilingual," a dedicatory inscription of c. 600 B.C. which is set out in two parallel versions, Ionic and Attic[5]; but this text at least suggests that Sigeum had fallen within the Attic sphere of influence by the time of Solon.

Of the Hellenistic dedications which call for notice we may mention a thank-offering set up at Orchomenus in Bœotia by twenty-three troopers safe home from Alexander's grand tour of Asia[6]; ex-votos by merchants or explorers who had survived the perils of the Red Sea and the Trogodytes,[7] and by "Petersen Sahibs" back from elephant hunts in Somaliland.[8]

A class of inscriptions which has a special importance consists of the signatures of Greek sculptors. Large numbers of these have been collected on such sites as Athens, Olympia, and Pergamum,[9] and the data thus obtained are a valuable guide in classifying the works

---

[1] DS 5; *Comptes rendus de l'Académie des Inscriptions*, 1924, p. 149.
[2] *B.M.* 930.   [3] H—H 6.   [4] *J.H.S.* 1905, p. 116.
[5] H—H 8; DS 2.   [6] M 1112.   [7] *O.G.I.* 69-71.
[8] *O.G.I.* 82, 86.
[9] E. Löwy, *Inschriften griechischer Bildhauer;* R—G 191-2; *Olymp.* 629-648; *Perg.* 132-146.

of the artists. Similarly the signatures of potters and designers on the fine Attic vases of the sixth and fifth centuries provide a means of sorting these wares into their proper groups.[1]

(iii) *Oracles.*—Registers of questions and answers may not have been kept at all the oracular seats; in any case it was not the custom to engrave them on durable material, except at Dodona, where leaden tablets containing the consultants' queries have been recovered. One Agis asks what has become of some mislaid or stolen bedding[2]; one Lysanias wants to know whether a child of his wife's is also his[3]; an unknown pilgrim seeks advice about investments in real property[4]; one Evander and his wife inquire what they must do to be happy ever after.[5] On a fourth-century stone from Trœzen we have both question and answer.[6] *Q.* "What doing shall I go to the god, having washed myself?" A. "Sacrifice to Heracles and Helios, having seen a favourable omen."

(iv) *Curses.*—A seamy side of Greek life is shown up by the maledictory inscriptions, of which large finds, dating from the fifth century onward, have been made on various sites, notably in Eubœa and Attica.[7] These texts were usually scrawled by semi-illiterates on strips of lead and despatched underground to the address of some infernal deity, who kept them safe against the coming of the modern excavator. The offences for

---

[1] J. C. Hoppin, *Handbook of Black-figure Vases; Handbook of Red-figure Vases.* A double check is provided by many Attic vases which carry the signature both of the Wedgwood who made the vessel and of the Flaxman who decorated it.

[2] M 851.   [3] M 850.   [4] M 846.
[5] M 845.   [6] DS 1159.

[7] A. Audollent, *Defixionum Tabellæ,* and *I.G.* III. pt. 3. Representative specimens in R—G 407-9, M 1319-29.

which their authors seek redress are mostly assault and
slander; one curious imprecation against a gay Lothario
appears to come from a jealous wife or spurned com-
petitor.[1] The punishments invoked are crudely physical: a common formula is "I bind down his tongue,
hands, feet, etc." But the earlier texts are sober and
business-like as compared with the fantastic rigmaroles
of later date, in which the entire host of hell is sum-
moned to do its collective worst. On an inscription from
Smyrna the curse anticipates the offence and makes the
punishment fit the crime: "do not annoy the sacred
fish, or may you come to a miserable end, being de-
voured of fish!"[2]

(8) *Economic transactions.* (i) *Deeds of sale.*—For ordinary market transactions the Greeks relied on oral
witnesses and did not make out receipts.[3] But in the
Hellenistic age registers of dealings in real property
were set up by public authorities. On a long inscription
from Tenos we read full descriptions of the objects
sold, the price and the security for payment.[4] On papyri
we find some deeds of sale of slaves, usually female
domestics.[5]

(ii) *Leases.*—These usually follow the lines laid down
in the renting of public or temple domains. A fifth century example from Olympia merely specifies that the
contract shall run for ever, the amount of the rent (in

[1] M 1321.
[2] M 728. For a similar imprecation on a tombstone, *cf.* R—G 381.
Curses upon tomb-riflers become painfully common under the Roman
Empire.
[3] From Egypt we have numerous orders to bankers, advices of payment,
and clearing-house transactions. (F. Preisigke, *Girowesen im griechisch-
römischen Aegypten*): But practically all these documents are of Roman date.
[4] *B.M.* 377; *I.J.G.* I, 7. *Cf.* also DS 968 (a similar list from Mytilene).
[5] *A.S.A.* XVIII. No. 3 (p. 164).

barley), and the penalty for default.[1] The texts from Egypt, which mostly refer to the sub-letting of military allotments to working tenants, do not as a rule prescribe minute rules as to the methods of cultivation; but in some cases the lessor is required to make improvements,[2] or at any rate to be in permanent residence,[3] and the clauses as to the incidence of the multifarious Ptolemaic imposts could not fail to be detailed. A good instance of an urban lease is given on a fourth-century text from Piræus, in which a syndicate of Athenians and metics hire a workshop and tenement on a repair lease and bind themselves under drastic penalties to pay a half-yearly rent.[4]

(iii) *Mortgages.*—Complete documents of this order are rare. The best examples relate to an estate at Arcesine on Amorgos which was secured to a creditor together with house, roof-tiles and all (*c.* 300 B.C.),[5] and to a latifundium containing several villages, which an officer of Antiochus I pledged to a temple-bank at Sardes.[6] Brief abstracts of mortgage deeds, inscribed on stone posts (ὅροι) which served to delimit the plot of land under lien, have been found abundantly in Attica and the Cyclades[7]. The following is a typical example: "limit of an estate sold for redemption to Calliteles' ἐρανισταί (friendly loan society) for 420 drachmas."[8]

---

[1] *Olymp.* 18.

[2] These usually consist of ἐμφυτεύσεις of olives and vines; the rules as to γῆ σπόριμος are simpler (e.g. Schubart-Kühn, 1263-1264; for a more elaborate lease of crop land, *cf.* P. Tebt. 105).

[3] *P. Petr.* II, 44, l. 19.   [4] R—G 130; DS 1216.   [5] DS 1200.

[6] *A.J.A.* 1912, p. 11. For another example *cf.* P. Petr. II, 46.

[7] R—G 352-8; *B.S.A.* XI, p. 70-1; M 1364-82; *I.J.G.* I, 8. The earliest extant specimens date from the fifth century. It is not unlikely that ὅροι made of wood had been set up before this time and continued in use outside of Attica and the Cyclades.   [8] M 1376.

(iv) *Loans.*—The usual Greek practice was to destroy paper i.o.u.s, and to erase entries on walls or boards, when repayment was made. Surviving loan-deeds are therefore not numerous. In one of the speeches attributed to Demosthenes we possess a good specimen of an Athenian "bottomry loan." In this instance two traders bent on a venture in the Black Sea borrowed 3,000 drachmas for the purchase of a cargo of wine; interest was reckoned at 22½ per cent., but the rate was to rise to 30 per cent. if the return journey was not begun before the end of the fine season.[1] From Egypt we have a document in which a woman money-lender places out her funds at the stiff rate of 24 per cent. yearly.[2] But more commonly the loans recorded on papyri are friendly transactions (in seed-corn or petty cash) on which no interest was charged[3]: no doubt they represent an attempt by the cultivators to eliminate the "gombeen man."

(v) *Sureties.*—As a rule the necessary clauses as to security were incorporated in the loan or mortgage deeds. Occasionally the guarantees were embodied in a separate document. In these cases the party who went bail expressly pledged his entire property.[4]

(vi) *Miscellaneous economic documents.*—A mixed assortment of other records of an economic character has been found in Egypt. We have already noticed the scheme for irrigation on Apollonius' estate (Ch. V, pp. 55-6); an-

---

[1] [Dem.] 35 §§ 10-13. For proof that this document is genuine, see Th. Thalheim, *Hermes*, 1888, p. 333 ff.

[2] F. Bilabel, *Griechische Papyri*, No. 2 (*Veröffentlichungen aus den badischen Papyrus-Sammlungen*, Vol. II).

[3] *P. Hibeh* 85-7; *Reinach* 8-16.

[4] *P. Petr.* III, 57-8; *Hibeh* 92-5; *Heidelberg* 3 (a soldier, Πέρσης τῆς Ἐπιγονῆς, stands surety for a friend in regard to payment of a tax).

other papyrus contains a contract for making bridges and canals, with full specifications.[1] Relating to the brisk Nile traffic we possess freighters' bills of lading, acknowledging receipt of food cargoes for transport to Alexandria on "The Queen" and other boats,[2] and lists of fares and freights.[3] There is no lack of household accounts and shopping lists, in some of which the merest pinches of salt and thimblefuls of oil are duly invoiced.[4]

(vii) *Trade marks.* A parallel to the stamps on government tiles which we have already noticed (Ch. V, p. 57) is furnished by inscriptions on pieces made by private contractors who in some cases apparently worked alongside the government kilns.[5] Another and a very large class of prints on clay ware consists of the names or monograms of manufacturers or eponymous officials stamped on wine jars destined for export. These inscribed amphoræ have been found on many sites, but their commonest provenance is Rhodes, Cnidus, Paros, or Thasos, and of these Rhodes provides by far the largest number.[6]

The most instructive of all the mercantile inscriptions are the trade marks on the bases of Attic vases exported to Italy. As the letter-forms of these are Ionic, we may infer that they were conveyed from Attica by Ionian merchants. On vases of the "fine red-figure" style these checkmarks are no longer found: after 480

---

[1] *P. Petr.* III, 43.   [2] *Lille* I, 21-4.   [3] *P. Petr.* III, 107.
[4] *P. Hibeh* 121; *P.S.I.* IV, 428-430.
[5] *Pergamon* 652-713.
[6] Of 114 stamped amphoræ in the Cairo Museum, 85 bear the name of a Rhodian ἐπώνυμος (J. G. Milne, *Greek Inscriptions in the Cairo Museum*); at Pergamum the number was 799 out of 882 (*Perg.* 766 ff.). *Cf.* also M. P. Nilsson, *Timbres amphoriques de Lindos.*

480 B.C., therefore, the Athenians did their own carrying.[1]

(viii) *Letters.*—Specimens of private correspondence are very plentiful among Greek papyri. Most of them date from the period of Roman rule, but as conditions of private life among the Egyptian Greeks were deliberately maintained in their pristine form, these later records may be used to illustrate life under the Ptolemies. The light which they cast upon Hellenism in foreign parts is most varied: their chief value lies in the information which they provide about family and social life and about the culture or semi-culture of the bourgeoisie and the poorer people.[2]

Some isolated scraps of correspondence on leaden tablets have been preserved. One of these contains a note from a man to his wife, telling her where to look for another lodging if evicted (fourth century).[3] The mass of letters purporting to come from the pen of Alexander which is preserved in the so-called "Alexander Romance" of pseudo-Callisthenes is self-evident fiction. The correspondence of other celebrities falls under the head of literary sources rather than of documents.

(ix) *School records.*—Official lists of pupils or prizewinners, and dedications to donors or emeriti teachers, have been recovered on the walls of school buildings.[4] But these are inferior in interest to the surviving specimens of pupils' work and play. Exercise books from

[1] R. Hackl, *Münchener archäologische Studien, Adolf Furtwängler gewidmet,* pp. 1-106.

[2] See the selection in P. Witkowski, *Epistulæ Græcæ Privatæ,* all of which are of Ptolemaic date. Isolated letters of various ages will be found in almost any collection of papyri.

[3] DS 1260. *Cf.* also DS 1259.

[4] See especially Th. Reinach, *Révue des études grecques,* 1893, p. 153 ff (inscriptions from Iasus).

Egypt show that schools do not alter much. The children learn their alphabet by intensive practice in selected letters and syllables; they receive moral edification from the Iliad or Æsop's fables; they are plagued with paradigms of verbs, and, such is the conservatism of schoolmasters, with exercises in the obsolete dual form.[1] Needless to say, Greek boys also tried their hand on school walls. On one long-suffering wall at Priene, which calls to mind the famous walls of Eton, Westminster, etc., the names of 732 scholars are scrawled, among them unflattering sobriquets such as Στρεψήλιος ("Sunflower"), Κονίορτος ("Dust-raiser"), and Βλάξ ("Lazybones").[2] A piece of juvenile humour survives in a list of Spartan ephors which includes Tyrtæus, Agis and Lysander.[3]

(x) *Graffiti.*—Next after the schoolboy, the most prolific scribbler was the globe-trotter. The temple walls and statues of Egypt in particular are defaced with Greek travellers' visiting cards, just as the Parthenon is now an address-book well filled with "Frankish" autographs.[4] Most of these scrawls ("Λύσανδρος ἥκω," etc.) have no special interest; but the earliest of them, a list of names of Ionian and Rhodian mercenaries in the service of Psammetichus II (c. 590 B.C.), who immortalised themselves on a colossus at Abu-Simbel

---

[1] J. G. Milne, *J.H.S.* 1908, p. 121 ff.; F. G. Kenyon, *ibid.* 1909, p. 29 ff. On the whole subject see E. Ziebarth, *Aus dem griechischen Schulwesen,* and *Aus der antiken Schule.*

[2] *Priene,* 313. *Cf.* also *Milet,* I. 7, 214-224.

[3] *Priene,* 316.

[4] See the collection of 671 specimens in P. Perdrizet and G. Lefèbvre, *Le Graffites grecs du Memnonion d'Abydos;* cf. also J. Baillet, *Mémoires de l'Institut français d'Archéologie orientale du Caire,* 1920. No. 1986 runs as follows: ἦ πού σε μήτηρ ἐκτὸς ὄντ' ἐπίσταται; See Tod, *Journal of Egyptian Archæology,* 1925, p. 256.

in Nubia, aptly illustrates Herodotus' story of the twenty-sixth dynasty and its unwelcome but indispensable Greek guests.[1]

One common type of modern graffito, the outpouring of a swelling heart, is scarcely represented among Greek inscriptions, unless we include in this class the numerous legends, "Μιλτιάδης καλός," " Ἀλκιβιάδης καλός," etc., which are found on Attic vases of the fifth century.[2] One good example is preserved on a portico at Priene, to which a love-lorn youth confides that "Chie is as the moon."[3]

Lastly, reference should be made to the marks of masons,[4] which may provide clues as to the date of a structure.

The graffiti of Greece include nothing that equals the famous "election posters" at Pompeii, but in numbers and variety they compare well with those of the Latin Corpus.

[1] H—H 3; DS 1. A similar inscription of 254 B.C. from Upper Egypt contains the names of fifteen Greek soldiers (O.G.I. 38).

[2] W. Klein, *Die griechischen Vasen mit Lieblingsinschriften*. Other historical names on Attic vases are Hipparchus, Megacles, Sicinnus, Callias, Leagrus (a great favourite), and Laches.

[3] *Priene*, 319.

[4] E.g. *Olymp.* 667-691.

CHAPTER IX

COINS

THE invention of coinage, for which credit is generally given to the Lydians, has been ascribed by some leading numismatists to the Greeks.[1] However this may be, the Greeks were certainly the first to put this invention to a thorough test. From the seventh century, when their first mints were opened, the practice of coinage spread rapidly over the Greek world, and by the fifth century it had become general. It has been estimated that at one time or other some 1,500 to 2,000 Greek mints issued money.[2] The metal most commonly used by Greek coiners was silver; but in the fourth century gold coins were issued by an increasing number of states, and in the third century bronze money came into common use.[3] The quantity and variety of coins issued from Greek mints were exceedingly great, and as the discovery both of single pieces and of entire hoards is constantly proceeding, the number of specimens available for study is not only large but grows apace.

Considered as historical documents, Greek coins have some defects and more merits. We shall consider the defects first.

[1] P. Gardner, *History of Ancient Coinage*, p. 67; E. Babelon, *Traité des monnaies grecques et romaines*, pt. II., vol. 1.   [2] P. Gardner, *op. cit.* p. 38.

[3] The earliest coins of Asia Minor were struck in a natural alloy of gold and silver known as electrum, which remained in use in certain mints, *e.g.* Cyzicus, to *c.* 400 B.C. The first gold coins were probably struck by Crœsus of Lydia. The gold "darics" of the Persian kings also circulated in Greece.

(1) Being eagerly sought after by experts and amateurs alike, Greek coins invite falsifications. Of the current forgeries few are skilful enough to deceive a practised eye, but the counterfeits of certain masters of the craft have long escaped detection.[1]

(2) The weights of Greek coins are less uniform than those of modern money, and in some cases it is difficult to decide on which standard they were struck. Not that the number of standards in use was excessively great. The earlier Greek pieces can all be reduced to two weight-systems, the Attic-Corinthian, with a standard silver didrachm of 130 grains, and the Argive-Æginetan, with a standard silver drachm of 90 grains.[2] In the Hellenistic age nearly all the Greek mints adopted the Attic-Corinthian standard, which Alexander had used for his imperial coinage.[3] In the intermediate period a few subsidiary systems, the "Lydian," "Phœnician," etc., were brought into use[4]; but the difficulty in classifying the coins lies not so much in the multiplicity of standards as in the imperfect manner in which many pieces conform to these standards. Some Greek cities deliberately struck a few grains above the

---

[1] *Cf.* G. F. Hill, *Becker the Counterfeiter* (1772-1830), and J. N. Svoronos on the recent forger Christodoulos (*J.I.A.N.* Vol. XX, p. 97 ff.).

[2] The didrachm of 130 grains was equal in weight to the "talent of gold," an old Greek unit of weighed currency which was deemed the equivalent in gold of an ox.

The drachm of 90 grains was the equivalent in silver of another old Greek weight-unit, the drachma of iron, which was a bunch of six iron bars or "obols" of specified weight.

[3] In 96 B.C. the Delphic Amphictyony decreed a forced currency for the tetradrachms of Athens, thus creating an international coin like the five-franc piece of the Latin Union (DS 729). The currency of Egypt and Rhodes and the "cistophori" of Ephesus and Pergamum, did not conform to the Attic standard.

[4] For different theories, see P. Gardner, *op. cit.* p. 24 ff., B. V. Head, *H.N.*, Introd.; C. T. Seltman, *Athens*, Ch. XV.

normal weights of the standard which they followed; others unheedingly caused a slight but progressive diminution of weight by restriking old coins; and Greek moneyers in general, like the makers of the early English pennies, took no trouble to adjust the weights of individual pieces.[1] Accordingly, though the weights of many coin-series have been satisfactorily explained and may safely be used to illustrate the monetary policy of the issuing state, there remain residual cases which are still *sub judice*; and while the "battle of the standards" which experts are still waging remains undecided, it would be a rash venture for the layman to base any arguments on the weights of coins.

(3) Greek coins of the pre-Roman period seldom carry any continuous legends. In the sixth century the practice arose of inscribing the name of the issuing state, either in full or, more usually, in abbreviation, and from the fourth century mint masters frequently engraved their names or monograms. But the earliest pieces carry no lettering at all, and on Greek coins of any century b.c. we miss the wealth of commemorative or propagandist legend which bedizen both Greek and Roman coins of the Roman Empire and convert these into miniature newspapers. A further deficiency which the historical student has particular reason to regret is the general absence of date-marks[2]: in quoting the dates assigned to Greek coins in such a handbook as

[1] On the correct way of averaging Greek coin-weights, see G. F. Hill, *N.C.*, 1924, p. 76 ff.

[2] The Hellenistic coins of Egypt and Syria in many cases carry a numeral which either indicates the year of the reign or, more commonly, the year of a given era (usually 312 B.C. in Syria and 311 B.C. in Egypt). See J. N. Svoronos, Τὰ Νομίσματα τοῦ Κράτους τῶν Πτολεμαίων, Vol. IV, and E. T. Newell, *The Seleucid Mint of Antioch*. The conclusions reached in Svoronos' book are still under dispute.

Head's *Historia Numorum*, we must remember that these usually rest on considerations of style or on stray pieces of circumstantial evidence, and that their accuracy is only approximate.

But the doubts and uncertainties arising out of these imperfections in Greek coins are being steadily reduced by the increasingly intensive study of their types and workmanship. So minute has this investigation become that expert numismatists have learnt to recognise on the face of coins the mint from which it proceeded and the dies from which it was struck. False coins are more surely detected; those of doubtful provenance have been assigned to their place of emission[1]; and undated series have been arranged in their proper sequence.[2]

Moreover, the defects of Greek coins are offset by some advantages which give them a high historical value.

(1) The many small mints of the Greek world had a far more checkered history than a single large mint of a centralised state could experience: not only did their rates of emission vary considerably, but on occasions they suspended issue altogether, only to resume at a more favourable moment. These vicissitudes of the Greek mints often serve to illustrate the political and economic history of the Greek states.

In the first place, the alacrity or tardiness with which the various Greek cities adopted coinage at the outset is a measure of their economic alertness or lethargy. As

---

[1] See especially C. T. Seltman, *Athens*, and the *Temple of Coins of Olympia*. In the former work an aristocratic mint in the city, a Pisistratid mint (at Laurium?), another Pisistratid mint in Thrace, and a colonial mint at Chalcis (506-490 B.C.) are distinguished.

[2] Obverse dies in Greek mints had a longer life than reverse dies. This fact assists us in fixing the serial order in which the reverse dies were used.

might be expected, the earliest towns to issue coins were the trading centres on either side of the Ægean Sea, most of which had established a mint by 600 B.C. On the other hand it was not until the fifth century that coinage became common in the interior of Peloponnesus, in Thessaly and north-western Greece, as also in Sicily; and Sparta held out against the new-fangled invention until about 300 B.C.

Similarly the spread of coinage among non-Greek peoples illustrates the growth of Greek influence among them. The Persians issued abundant quantities of gold and silver from the days of Darius I, perhaps even in the days of Cyrus. The Phœnicians held out against coinage until the fourth century; but Hindoo princes began to strike (on Macedonian and Athenian patterns) soon after Alexander's invasion, and in the second and first centuries the Indo-Parthian and Indo-Scythian dynasties issued Greek types on a considerable scale.[1] In the west the Etruscans struck silver and bronze coins towards the end of the fifth century; the Romans issued their earliest bronze about 350 B.C., and their first silver some thirty years later.[2] The Carthaginians did not strike until the fourth century, and their earliest pieces, being struck in Sicily on a Syracusan pattern, were probably intended for their mercenary forces in the Greek wars rather than for their own traders. The scanty Spanish issues reflect Roman rather than Greek influence; on the other hand the copious emissions of the Gallic tribes (from c. 300 B.C.) are

[1] For details, see Head, *H.N.*, p. 835; V. A. Smith, *Catalogue of the Coins in the Indian Museum, Calcutta*, Vol. I, 5 ff.

[2] The first Roman denarii were struck at Capua; the mint at Rome did not emit silver before 268 B.C.

mostly imitations of the coins of Philip II of Macedon. The Philip type was also reproduced in Britain (first century B.C.), but "quantum mutatus ab illo."

Again, the varying fortunes of Greek mints often reflect some political change, e.g. the imposition or removal of control over a smaller state by an imperial power. Such control indeed was never exercised by Sparta over her dependents, but in the Athenian empire after 450 B.c. only a few favoured mints such as Thasos, Lampsacus, Cyzicus, and Chios were allowed to remain in operation.[1] Conversely, successful rebellion from Athens was usually celebrated by new issues, and in the fourth century coinage again became common in the Ægean area, the Athenians not daring again to intervene. The history of the Bœotian mints is a running commentary on the history of the Bœotian League: it is no mere accident that Thebes established a monopoly of coinage c. 450 B.c. and resumed it after a temporary interruption from c. 375 to 330 B.c. The greater or lesser degree of centralisation in the Greek federal states of the fourth, third, and second centuries is also reflected in their coinage. The Ætolian League suppressed the mints of its constituents; the Achæan League merely imposed a uniform type and weight upon the constituents' issues.[2]

The varying policies of the Hellenistic monarchs towards their dependents find similar illustration. In Egypt and its outlying possessions only Ptolemaic coins

---

[1] P. Gardner, J.H.S. 1913, p. 147 ff. The decree of c. 420 B.C. (referred to in Ch. IV. p. 43) marks the final stage in the suppression of local mints. A good instantia ex contrario is furnished by the abundant coinage of Melos, the only independent island (R. Jameson, Revue numismatique, 1909, p. 188 ff.).
[2] M. Caspari, J.H.S. 1917, p. 168 ff.

were allowed to circulate[1]; under the Pergamene and Seleucid kings the vassal cities commonly struck bronze and sometimes silver.[2] To these instances may be added some special cases in which an ephemeral mint struck a short series on account of some transient political reason. Themistocles' pieces at Magnesia, the coins of the Arcadian federation of 370 B.C. and of their clients the Pisatans (364 B.C.), and the commemorative issues of the Delphic Amphictyony after the Sacred War are cases in point.

Arguments from the quantity of extant coins of any particular issue require to be stated with caution, for the ratio of coins surviving to coins issued may vary greatly from case to case. But expansions or contractions of currency may be taken as proved when coin finds increase or diminish rapidly, and may therefore be used to throw light upon the march of history. The rapid rise in the output of Athenian coinage under the Pisistratids throws into relief the wealth and the commercial activity of these tyrants.[3] The abundance of fourth-century coins from Cyzicus suggests the growth of trade with the interior of Asia up the Rhyndacus or Sangarius valley. The immense output of Alexander's mints is an obvious result of his raids of bullion in the gorgeous yet secretive East. Since one of the chief consumers of specie in the ancient world was the soldier on active service, it is worth inquiring whether other spurts by Greek mints may not stand in connexion with special military efforts.

[1] Coins of Ptolemaic type were struck at branch mints in Cyrene, Cyprus and Palestine.—Svoronos, *op. cit.* Vol. IV.

[2] On the Pergamene coinage, see H. v. Fritze, *Abh. Berl. Ak.* 1910, p. 1 ff. The silver "cistophori" of Ephesus and Pergamum are good instances of local coinage.   [3] Seltman, *Athens*, p. 43-4.

(2) The production of coins in a metal previously unused may stand in connexion with some historical event. The emergency issues of gold and bronze at Athens towards the end of the fifth century were plainly consequent upon the loss of the silver mines at Laurium to the Peloponnesians. The gold pieces struck at Athens and Thebes at the beginning of the fourth century sent bullion as well as "golden archers" across the Ægean, or that the archers were melted down for re-issue with Greek types. The more general emission of gold *c.* 350 B.C. recalls to mind the dispersion of the Delphic treasures during the Sacred War, and the subsequent establishment of gold as a collateral, rather than an auxiliary, of silver is a visible result of Alexander's Anabasis.[1] The most notorious instance of the debasement of coinage by Greek moneyers, the issue of copper tetradrachms with a covering film of silver or tin by Dionysius I of Syracuse, may be taken as evidence that the Carthaginians had cut him off from the mines of Spain. But instances of depreciation are rare among Greek coins. Competition between various mints and the briskness of inter-state commerce acted as checks upon such fraud. Moreover, those states which had power to secure a forced currency for bad money usually possessed enough foresight or integrity to eschew such malpractices. The Athenians displayed exemplary honesty in this respect, and their high standard was maintained by most of the Hellenistic kings.[2]

[1] The ratio of value between gold and silver, which in the fifth century had stood at 14:1, sank progressively to 12:1 and 10:1.—Th. Reinach, *L'Histoire par les monnaies*, p. 44; P. Gardner, *op. cit.* p. 31 ff.
[2] On the alleged "crying down" of the Athenian didrachms by Hippias, see Seltman, *Athens*, p. 77-8. The suspicions which used to attach to Themistocles' coinage at Magnesia have been proved to be unfounded (R. Weil *Corolla Numismatica: Num smatic Essays in Honour of B. V. Head*, p. 306 ff.).

(3) Greek coins as a rule passed freely from one Greek state to another, and were accepted outside Greece as currency or keepsakes. Their distribution, therefore affords some insight into the direction and volume of Greek trade. In the numerous hoards of fifth and fourth century date which have been unearthed in Sicily and S. Italy the pieces of Athens and Corinth predominate, and of the fifth-century money found at Naucratis[1] eight-ninths was Athenian. Greek coins of the sixth century and onward are found in S. Russia as far as Kiev; specimens of fourth-century type occur sporadically in the Danube lands; in Gaul the Macedonian "Philips," and the pieces of Massilia, Emporiæ, and Rhoda from *c.* 300 B.C. become common, though only isolated finds have occurred near the Atlantic seaboard.[2] The Persian Empire and Carthage on the other hand had no appetite for Greek money.

(4) The inscriptions on Greek coins, though brief, are not without historical interest. The appearance of the legend *Αἰτναίων* on coins of Catana illustrate the second foundation of that town under the name of "Ætna" by Hiero of Syracuse.[3] The legends *Σύ(βαρις)* on a coin obverse of Poseidonian type and *Ποσ(ειδώνια)* on a revenue of Sybarite type, form a curious chiasmus which clearly proves a monetary alliance between the towns in question. The substitution of "*Θουρίων*" for *Σύβαρι(ς)* on Sybarite coins of *c.* 450 B.C. is a reminder of Athenian intervention in Italian affairs.[4] The

---

[1] B. V. Head, in Petrie-Gardner, *Naukratis* I, p. 63-66.
[2] The "Farthest West" of Greek coin-hoards is the island of Jersey. On the diffusion of Greek money in Gaul, see A. Blanchet, *Revue numismatique belge*, 1913, p. 308 ff.
[3] G. F. Hill, *Historical Greek Coins*, Nos. 21-22.
[4] *Ibid.* nos. 24-6.

letters συμ(μαχικόν) on coins of Byzantium, Ephesus, Samos, Iasus, Cnidus and Rhodes (c. 390 or 380 B.C.) plainly betoken some alliance, though its details are as yet uncertain.[1] The name 'Επαμι(νώνδας) on Bœotian money may be taken as evidence that the generals of the Bœotian League also served as mint-masters.[2] The Phocians' coins inscribed ὀνυμάρχου and φαλαίκου, and the Delphic issue with the word 'Αμφικτιόνων, show up the vicissitudes of the Sacred War.[3] The intrusion of "βα" or "βασιλεύς" on coins of the Diadochi is a sure sign that the last stage in the transition from satrap to monarch has been traversed.[4] Lastly, the recurrent legend "Φιλέλλην" on coins of Parthia from c. 150 B.C. reveals the solicitude of the Arsacids for their revenue-producing Greek subjects in Mesopotamia; and the gradual substitution of native for Greek words and lettering on the Indo-Parthian mintages prove the ⌐low extrusion of Hellenism from India.[5]

(5) Chief of all, the historical importance of Greek coins lies in their types, which are unsurpassed in their variety and reflect current events as faithfully as do the stamps of certain modern states.

The earliest types on Greek money were commonly the personal emblems of the noble families who issued them: in some cases they seem to have been identical

[1] *Ibid.* nos. 32-33.

[2] *Ibid.* no. 36.

[3] *Ibid.* nos. 50-52.

[4] The list of βασιλεῖς includes the upstarts Agathocles and Hiero at Syracuse. On the other hand the royal title does not appear on coins of Pergamum before the reign of Eumenes II (197-159 B.C.). The title of king had previously appeared on the money of Mausolus and his father.

[5] See V. A. Smith, *op. cit.*, and R. B. Whitehead, *Catalogue of the Coins in the Punjab Museum, Lahore*, Vol. I.

with their seal-marks and the devices on their shields.[1]
Thus on the early Attic coins we may perhaps recognise
the cart-wheel of the Butadæ, the "Isle of Man"
symbol of the Alcmæonidae, and a cantering horse
which is possibly derived from Pisistratus' coat of
arms.[2] But these family types presently made way for
emblems which speak for the entire body politic. Thus
at Athens the head of Athens displaces the old aristocratic devices and remains the standing type on Athenian money for century after century. The change,
significantly enough, was first made on the coins of
Pisistratus.

Of the manifold ways in which coin types illustrate
the history of the issuing state only a few examples can
here be given. The appearance of identical types on the
mintage of different cities is good evidence of political
relations. The standing Corinthian type of a Pegasus
and helmeted Athena recurs on the money of the
Corinthian colonies, with the significant exception of
Corcyra, which unlike the others maintained her inde-
pendence. Similarly Anaxilas of Rhegium struck coins
of identical type on either side of the Straits of Messi-
na.[3] When Thero of Acragas captured Himera the
Acragantine crab fastened itself upon the money of the
conquered town.[4] The intrusion of the tripod of Croton
upon coins of Sybaris, Temesa, Caulonia, Poseidonia
and Zancle (c. 460 B.C.) suggests a short-lived Cro-

[1] See G. Macdonald, *Coin Types*, p. 49 ff. One archaic coin from Asia
Minor bears the inscription φαένος ἐμὶ σῆμα ("I am the badge of Phanes")
—P. Gardner, *Types of Greek Coins*, pl. 4, n. 8. A few early Greek types
seem to be derived from Minoan gems (A. J. Evans, *J.H.S.*, 1912, p. 294).

[2] Seltman, *Athens*, Chs. III-VI.

[3] Hill, *op. cit.* Nos. 15-17. On the complicated story of Anaxilas' coinage
see C. H. Dodd, *J.H.S.* 1908, p. 56 ff.

[4] Hill, nos. 18-19.

tonian empire at the time of the Pythagorean ascendancy. Among fourth-century types in the western Greek states those of Syracuse and Tarentum are particularly eloquent. The sudden but brief apparition of the Corinthian Pegasus on the coins of Syracuse commemorates the meteoric advent of Timoleon; similarly the intervention of foreign *condottieri* in the wars of Tarentum is betokened by a type in which Taras, the legendary founder of the town, gazes mournfully upon an empty helmet, viz., that of the fallen Spartan king Archidamus; and on a later piece a head of the Zeus of Dodona and an elephant indicate the presence of king Pyrrhus.[1]

The issues of Alexander mark a new departure in Greek coin types, in that they bear the head of the reigning monarch. Since the heads previously delineated on Greek money were exclusively those of gods and heroes, we may take this portraiture of Alexander as proof of his apotheosis. The impression made by Alexander upon the Greek world is shown by the persistence of his portrait as a coin-type, for it recurs not only on the issues of the Diadochi but on those of numerous city states for a long time after his death.

The evolution of the succession-states can be traced in the types of the Diadochi no less than in their coin-legends. By degrees the head of the reigning king supplants that of Alexander, and with each fresh ruler a new type usually appears.[2] A portrait series of parti-

[1] B. V. Head, *The Coinage of Syracuse*, p. 30 and pts. 6-7; A. J. Evans, *The Horsemen of Tarentum*, pp. 157-8.

[2] Hill, nos. 61-63 (Ptolemy I); no. 70 (Seleucus); no. 73 (Philetacrus of Pergamum). The Pergamene coins retained the founder's portrait down to the time of Eumenes II (197-159 B.C.). In Egypt the type of Ptolemy I was retained on one principal series until 195 B.C.

cular interest is found on the coins of the Greek kings of Bactria and India in the third and second centuries B.C. These are our chief source of information concerning these outposts of Hellenism.[1] The gradual Mongolisation of the kings' features illustrates the process by which the Greek element was absorbed by its Oriental environment. Among the later Greek types which commemorate notable achievements by Greek monarchs we may mention a horseman pursuing an elephant on a coin of Alexander (referring to his victory over king Porus)[2]; a victory on the prow of a ship, on a piece of Demetrius (this figure is a memorial of one of Demetrius' naval triumphs)[3]; and a victory and trophy on the money of Agathocles (on the occasion of his victories in Africa).[4]

Not only did the main types of Greek coins serve to advertise the events of the day, but subsidiary devices often gave additional hints. On the money of Athens from the early fifth century onward Athena's helmet is graced with a garland—in memory of Marathon. On the Syracusan decadrachms of Gelo the bottom segment is occupied by a lion courant,[5] and on a later issue of the same series a set of prize armour is shown.[6] The lion symbolises Carthage, the trophy refers to the Assinaria, the games that commemorated the great Syracusan victory over Athens. On an early issue of Ptolemy I an anchor and the head of Bucephalus are shown in miniature. These were the arms of Seleucus,

[1] See the *Cambridge History of India*, Vol. I. Ch. XVII, (by G. Macdonald), and Ch. XXII (by E. J. Rapson).
[2] Head, *H.N.* p. 833.
[3] Hill, no. 69.   [4] *Ibid.*, no. 66.
[5] *Ibid.*, no. 20.
[6] *Ibid.*, no. 29.

which here symbolise his momentary alliance with Ptolemy.[1]

Finally, historians as well as artists may learn a lesson from the amazing development in the style of Greek coin types from the muddled devices of the archaic pieces to the decadrachms which Cimon[2] and Euænetus designed for Syracuse, to the gold didrachms of Tarentum,[3] and to king Lysimachus' portraits of Alexander.[4] To study a series of types from the earliest to the best period of Greek numismatic art is perhaps the quickest way of realising the progress of Greek civilisation.

APPENDIX. To this chapter we may annex a brief notice of the inscribed tablets and discs of bronze or clay which served as checks in law-courts, theatres, etc. The best known specimens are the fourth-century dicasts' tickets from Athens, which gave the dicast's name and the serial number of his division in the dicasts' roll.[5] From Athens we also have bronze theatre-checks, with a number denoting the block to which they admitted, and similar clay vouchers from Mantinea.[6] But these specimens are hardly equal to the fine "panis et circenses" tesseræ of the Roman Empire.

[1] Svoronos, Νομίσματα τοῦ Κράτους τῶν Πτολεμαίων, Vol. IV, pp. 42-3.
[2] Hill, no. 29.
[3] Evans, *The Horsemen of Tarentum*, pl. V.
[4] *Ibid.*, no. 71.
[5] H—H, 151.
[6] Svoronos, *J.I.A.N.* Vol. I, p. 37 ff., 107 ff; *I.G.V.* 2, 323.

CHAPTER X

IN the chapter on coins we dealt with a class of document whose historical value did not depend solely or even chiefly upon its written texts. In this chapter we shall consider the miscellaneous material remains which convey no written message. These, too, if properly questioned, may be made to yield historical information.

(1) *Remains of towns.*—The peculiar circumstances which preserved Pompeii as a historical museum have not been repeated on Greek soil, and most of the ancient Greek cities have been subjected to destruction by the later occupants of adjacent settlements, who have picked away the old buildings and used up their stones. A more or less clean sweep has thus been made of Athens (the lower city[1]), Corinth, Syracuse, Alexandria, Antioch.[2] Of the surviving remnants the greater portion belongs to the Hellenistic and Roman strata, and is to be found in Asia Minor rather than in the Greek homeland. But in the last fifty years much new information about Greek towns has been acquired by excavation. Not to mention the prehistoric cities, which fall outside the scope of this work, many important sites

---

[1] Extensive excavations in the lower city of Athens have recently been commenced by the American School of Archæology.

[2] At Antioch a large portion of the ancient city wall has been fetched away during the last fifty years only.

of the historic period have been unearthed. In Greece Proper the Athenian Acropolis, Delphi, Olympia, Sparta, Megalopolis and the Asclepieum of Epidaurus have been systematically explored; Delos and Thera among the island settlements; Miletus, Ephesus, Priene and Pergamum in Asia Minor; Naucratis in Egypt; Cumæ and Gela in the West. These and other excavations have yielded much new knowledge about the construction of Greek towns and their history.

The first known instance of systematic town-planning in Greece occurs at Miletus as reconstructed after 479 B.C.; but it was not until the Hellenistic age that the scientific laying-out of town sites became general. Greek cities differed from Italian ones in that they usually had but one wide street running along the major axis, without a "decumanus" to intersect it, and they were less prone to sacrifice practical utility to decorative effect.[1]

Fortifications.—Few of the surviving specimens are of earlier date than 500 B.C., and not until the fourth century do they give much evidence of scientific planning or uniform care in construction. The Long Walls of Athens and Corinth and Themistocles' ramparts at the Piræus have disappeared. The surviving walls round the Athenian Acropolis, which were built in 480–460 B.C., had no military purpose, but were only part of a scheme for levelling the summit of the citadel.[2] Fragments from three of the rings round the lower city are still visible near the Dipylon Gate on the N.W. sector. (i) Themistocles' wall, with hastily assembled

[1] See especially A. v. Gerkan, *Griechische Städteanlagen.*
[2] For details, see E. A. Gardner, *Ancient Athens*, Ch. II.

foundations and a plinth of polygonal masonry on which courses of sun-dried brick could be rapidly thrown up. (ii) The reconstruction of Conon's time (B.C. 393 ff.), of similar plan but better workmanship. (iii) Lycurgus' lines (B.C. 338), built throughout in square ashlar.[1] At Piræus the lining of masonry and rubble core of Conon's reconstruction partly survives. Good specimens of fifth-century work may be seen at the Attic border-forts of Phyle and Eleutheræ. In Bœotia the lower courses of the wall of Platæa, in good square masonry, are still visible, and in Ætolia there are numerous remains of walls and towers which no doubt did good service in the days of the Macedonian invasions.[2] In Peloponnesus the lower courses of Mantinea's fortifications, with overlapping curtains at each gate, and the giant stride of Epaminondas' finely made wall up the slope of Ithome, are visible marks of the policy by which Sparta was built in and reduced to impotence (c. 370 B.C.). At Sparta itself there is no trace of walls previous to those of King Nabis (c. 200 B.C.). Among the towns of the western Greeks Selinus retains part of the reconstructed rampart of Hermocrates (B.C. 407), and at Syracuse there are still whole acres of Dionysius' fortifications at the apex of the Epipolæ plateau, the strongest point of the strongest fortress of ancient times. Of the Hellenistic fortifications special mention is due to the walls of Ephesus and Heraclea-on-Latmus. The latter, with their high parapets and covered towers spanning the width of the wall,

---

[1] E. A. Gardner, *Ancient Athens*, ch. 2; A. Frickenhaus, *Die Mauren Athens im vierten Jahrhundert v. Chr.*; F. Noack, *A.M.* 1907, p. 123 ff., 473 ff.

[2] W. J. Woodhouse, *Ætolia*.

may be taken as a type of the fortresses built to resist the new artillery of the Hellenistic age.[1]

Public buildings.—The remnants of these are just sufficient to indicate their usual style of architecture. A round theatre at Megalopolis, with accommodation for 10,000, and a square theatre at Priene, with seats for 640, may be taken as the types, large and small, of a place of popular assembly. The arrangements on the Pnyx at Athens are not clear, as only the speaker's platform remains, and the ground now slopes downward instead of rising from this. At Megalopolis a covered and colonnaded building alongside of the place of assembly served as the Council Hall. At Miletus the Council House was built on similar lines, but had a small theatre adjoining it (*c.* 175 B.C.). A specimen of a Greek Town Hall has been discovered at Priene. This was not, like the Prytaneum at Athens, a round building, but resembled a private house with a courtyard. Of Hellenistic palaces we have no remains except at Pergamum. The residence built here by Eumenes II was simply a large private house.

Libraries.—In the Palace Quarter of Pergamum were found the remains of the famous library-building. In addition to four large rooms for reading or storing books, this contained an open terrace where readers could breathe fresh air and dispel cobwebs.

Theatres.—The existing remains throw little light on the construction of theatres in the classical age of the Greek drama. The fifth-century auditoria, being made of wood, have disappeared, and the stage-buildings have

---

[1] See F. Krischen, *Milet* III, pt. 2. For Greek harbour fortifications, see K. Lehmann-Hartleben, *Die antiken Hafenanlagen des Mittelmeeres,* especially Ch. IV (*Klio, Beiheft* XIV).

been more or less obliterated by reconstructions. At Athens the auditorium as rebuilt by Lycurgus (*c.* 330 B.C.), with a seating capacity of 17-20,000, survives in tolerably good condition; the stage is mostly of Roman date. The largest remaining theatres are the Hellenistic buildings at Miletus, Ephesus and Pergamum; the best preserved structure is at the Asclepieum of Epidaurus. The last-named theatre is remarkable for its perfect symmetry and for the full circle of its orchestra (*c.* 300 B.C.).

Racecourses.—At Olympia the stadium has not been recovered; but at Delphi, Epidaurus, and Miletus racecourses with rising tiers of seats for the onlookers are preserved. At Delphi the grooved sill at the starting-point still shows up clearly.

Aqueducts.—The earliest surviving specimens all date back to the age of the tyrants. The well-house of the Cypselids on Acrocorinth, the conduits of Theagenes at Megara, of Pisistratus at Athens, and of Gelo or Hiero at Syracuse are partly preserved; and the tunnel which Polycrates' engineer Eupalinus drove through the rock near Samos can still be traversed by a "well-girt" and flexible person. Among later Greek aqueducts it is not always easy to distinguish those of Hellenistic and of Roman date. Of the undoubtedly Hellenistic ones the most remarkable is at Pergamum, with bronze pipes constructed to resist a high pressure.

Private houses.—The only surviving examples which convey an adequate idea of structure and decoration are the Hellenistic residences at Delos and Priene. The normal pattern of these recalls that of the Pompeian peristyle, and the decorations resemble those of the earlier residences at Pompeii. But the variations in detail are considerable.

Temples.—The more important of these were protected against dilapidation during pagan antiquity, and some which were eventually converted into churches or mosques retained their immunity in later times.[1] Consequently the remains of Greek temple architecture are considerable. For the historian as for the artist the shrines on the Acropolis of Athens are of the first importance. The Parthenon, whose foundations were laid in the sixth century, and the Erechtheum, which replaced Athena's oldest temple, illustrate many a page from the history of Athens.[2] Among other temples which are still partly standing we may mention the sanctuary of Aphæa on Ægina, a monument to Æginetan prowess at Salamis, and the beautiful shrine of Apollo at Bassæ, built by Ictinus, the architect of the Parthenon, in memory of the plague of 430 B.C., which Apollo was believed to have averted from the neighbouring town of Phigalea. At Olympia the foundation only of the great fifth-century temple of Zeus remains, but the walls and columns of the Heræum, part of which dates back to the seventh or eighth century, are still in fair preservation. At Delphi the base of the fourth-century temple of Apollo, and the underground *adytum* where the oracles were delivered, have been unearthed. At Sparta parts of the temple of Athena Chalciœcus, in which Pausanias was starved, and of the shrine of Artemis Orthia, together with the famous

---

[1] The Parthenon has served in turn as a church and a mosque, and the so-called Theseum was used for many centuries by Christian worshippers. At Syracuse an archaic temple forms part of the present cathedral.

[2] E. A. Gardner, *op. cit.* chs. 4-8.

altar, are still preserved. Among the numerous remains of temples in the West special mention is due to those of Acragas, which were built with the labour of Carthaginian captives. To this list we may add Ictinus' Hall of Initiation at Eleusis, whose processional floor and raised auditorium are in part preserved, and the "treasuries" for trophies and ex-votos at Olympia and Delphi. At the latter site the treasury of Corinth, which Phrygian and Lydian kings enriched, and the Massilian storehouse, where Roman spoils were lodged, have perished; but the Athenian repository for the spoils of Marathan has been recently rebuilt with the original stones.

Tombs.—Funeral monuments of kings and grandees which play such a large part in Egyptian archæology, are as yet of little importance to the student of Greek history. Of the Mausoleum nothing is left save the precious but scanty remnants in the British Museum; the burial places of Alexander and the Hellenistic kings still await discovery. The historical sculptures on some of the more sumptuous tombs, and the pottery found inside them, will be discussed later on (pp. 119, 121 ff.). The numerous graves of common people require no detailed notice. It is useful to remember that Dorians laid out their dead facing eastward, and Ionians westward; but it is dangerous to draw far-reaching conclusions from the alternate practices of inhumation and cremation, for these afford no sure test of race or culture.[1]

Mine workings.—An examination of the Attic silver mines at Laurium has shown that these were exploited by a multitude of small working parties who drove their

[1] See especially H. Dragendorff in Hiller v. Gärtringen, *Thera*, p. 83 ff.

adits without any common plan of exploitation. The only evidence of methodical prospecting on a large scale is to be found in some deep trial shafts, possibly the work of the tyrants, which led to the discovery of the really productive lode at the "third contact."[1]

(2) *Sculptures and paintings.*—Many of the largest and best Greek works of art served to commemorate past events, but they usually drew their subjects from the mythological rather than the historical past, and among the Greek monuments there is nothing whose historical value equals that of the monuments of Nineveh or Egyptian Thebes, or of Trajan's column at Rome. Of the larger sculptured groups the only ones that require mention here are the frieze of the temple of Athena Nike at Athens, with its representation of a combat between Greeks and Persians (c. 450 B.C.), and the famous Parthenon frieze, in which the pageantry of the Panathenæa goes marching on.[2] Of historical frescoes none have survived; but in the famous mosaic from Pompeii which depicts Alexander and Darius at the battle of Issus[3] we have no doubt a replica of a commemorative painting; and from the careful description of the antiquarian Pausanias and the individual figures on contemporary vase-paintings it has been possible to reconstruct Polygnotus' "Battle of Marathon" in the Stoa Pœcile at Athens (c. 460 B.C.).[4] Of single statues we still possess a number that were set up as war memorials. A recently discovered statue at Sparta, representing a warrior in a heroic attitude, and executed c. 470–460

---

[1] E. Ardaillon, *Les Mines du Laurion*, ch. 3, pt. 2.
[2] E. A. Gardner, *op. cit.* p. 322 ff.
[3] Mau-Kelsey, *Pompeii*, p. 288.
[4] C. Robert, *Die Marathonschlacht in der Poikile.*

B.C., has been plausibly identified with Leonidas.[1] From the age of the Macedonian and Hellenistic warlords the chief surviving monuments are the "Lion of Chæronea," probably a Macedonian memorial, and the Pergamene statue popularly known as the "Dying Gladiator," which in reality represents a Galatian chieftain. In addition to these monuments of kings and captains we may mention the "Tomb of Dexileos" at Athens, on which is engraved a battle scene from the Corinthian War (c. 394 B.C.),[2] and the gorgeous "Sidon Sarcophagus,"[3] on which one piece represents Macedonians fighting Persians and another shows Alexander hunting with a Persian escort.

Of surviving historical sculptures by far the largest class consists of portraits of celebrities. From the sixth century onward it became customary in Greek states to reward public merit with a statue or bust, and in the Hellenistic period the rise of a biographic literature created a considerable demand for portraits among private customers. Unfortunately many of the portraits which we possess carry no inscription or only a late and unauthentic legend, so that their identification is a matter of doubt. Some figures, e.g., Homer and Hesiod, Harmodius and Aristogiton, are as fanciful as Dürer's Charlemagne or the English kings on the rood screen at York; and the prototype of the Delphi Charioteer, if indeed this famous statue is a portrait, remains uncertain.[4] We are left to choose between two dissimilar busts of Herodotus and of Plato; the seated statue commonly

[1] A. M. Woodward, *J.H.S.* 1925, p. 215.
[2] E. A. Gardner, *op. cit.* p. 466.
[3] M. Collignon, *Histoire de la sculpture grecque*, II, p. 405-11.
[4] See Ch. V, p. 64.

called "Aristotle" more probably represents some
Roman worthy, and the identity of the Lateran "Sophocles" has recently been called in question.[1] But no
doubt exists as to the statue of Mausolus, which is from
the Mausoleum[2]; our two signed busts of Pericles bear
a convincing likeness,[3] and there is a clear resemblance
between our twenty-five "Euripides," thirty-two "Socrates" and thirty-two "Demosthenes"; our "Alexan-
ders" and other Hellenistic portraits (e.g., of Seleucus,
Pyrrhus, Philetaerus) are proved authentic by the corresponding coin types.[4]

(3) *Small objects.*—The quantity of small finds at our
disposal is considerable. Their provenance is mostly not
from houses, whose furniture was scanty and consisted
largely of perishable material, but from temples, where
objects of more costly and lasting fabric were conse-
crated, and from tombs, which vied with temples as
repositories of precious and durable ware. The only
objects that require discussion here are those of metal
and clay, and of these the ceramic ware is much the
more important.

Of the metals found on Greek sites the commonest
is bronze. But the finds in this material, being mostly
domestic furniture, are not of high historical value. The
most important from the historian's point of view are
the pins and brooches which abound at early sites with
a Dorian population, e.g., the Argive Heræum, Ægi-

---

[1] See the discussion between Th. Reinach and F. Studniczka in *J.H.S.*
1922-24.
[2] Now in the British Museum.
[3] One of these is in the British Museum.
[4] On the whole subject, see especially J. Bernoulli, *Griechiscke Ikonographie.* For a new portrait of Socrates, *cf.* H. B. Walters, *J.H.S.* 1925,
p. 255 ff.

na, Sparta, and Thera, where the Doric unsewn chiton was worn until the sixth century. At the Argive Heræum a bunch of iron bars was found which undoubtedly had served as money and may be the very pieces which King Pheidon dedicated.[1] The other iron objects have mostly rusted away, and of iron armour not enough remains to throw much light on Greek warfare.[2] Gold and silver finds, except in the form of coins, are rare on most sites of the historic period, where the tomb riflers evidently met with better fortune than at prehistoric Mycenæ. But in S. Russian tombs of the fifth to the third century, both Greek and native, astonishing quantities of gold and silver ornaments have been discovered. These finds are of high importance for the study of Greek art and betoken the great prosperity of the Scythian coastlands during the lull between the Cimmerian and the Sarmatian storms.[3]

On Greek sites down to the fourth century ceramic wares constitute by far the most copious finds. Large quantities of pottery have also been discovered in other Mediterranean lands. Greek clay ware was not provided with manufacturers' marks like the Roman *terra sigillata*. Hence their provenance and in some cases their date is a matter of doubt. A troublesome uncertainty exists as to the origin of the "geometric "pottery which was common in Greece from the eleventh to the eighth century. This is usually regarded as an importation which first came tò Greece with the Dorian Inva-

[1] C. T. Seltman, *Athens,* p. 118.
[2] For a description of the iron arrow-heads of the Persian troops at Marathon, see E. J. Forsdyke, *Proceedings of the Society of Antiquaries,* 1920, p. 146 ff.
[3] M. Rostovtseff, *Iranians and Greeks in Southern Russia.* The finds extend as far as Kieff. The richest of all the tombs were those of Panticapæum.

sion; but some competent archæologists regard it as a survival of a prehistoric fabric. Another standing puzzle is provided by the "proto-Corinthian" pottery, a well-made and widely diffused ware of the eighth and seventh centuries. This was probably traded from Corinth, but was almost certainly not made there. It may have come from Sicyon or Argos, but opinion among experts remains divided.[1] A fabric which occurs in plenty at Naucratis and S. Russia has naturally been given the name of "Milesian," but a good case has been made out for deriving it from Rhodes.[2] But as a rule Greek pottery carries trustworthy marks of its age and provenance. The texture and colour of the clay sometimes reveal the origin of the vase, and an excellent criterion is provided by the signatures of the artists and the various legends inserted on the field. On the strength of their letter-forms certain classes of pottery are now confidently described as Corinthian, Chalcidian, Melian, etc., and there can be no doubt about the large amphoræ on which we read "τῶν ᾿Αθήνηθεν ἄθλων." For the dating of vases we possess some fixed points of reference. The specimens found at Naucratis are anterior to the conquest of Egypt by the Persians (c. 525 B.C.); and those which were excavated from the "Perserschutt" on the Acropolis, i.e., the pockets into which the Athenians dumped the débris caused by Xerxes' devastations, cannot be later than 480 B.C. Furthermore, the development of technique in making and decorating certain classes of vases was so continuous that these can be accurately grouped in their

[1] For a recent discussion, cf. K. Johansen, Les vases sicyoniens.
[2] For recent statements of opposite views, see H. Prinz, Funde aus Naukratis (Klio, Beiheft VII), and Miss E. R. Price, J.H.S. 1924, p. 180 ff.

serial order, and thus provided at least with a relative date.

The historical interest of Greek ceramic ware rests in the first instance on the paintings with which the better class of fabrics was usually decorated. These pictures illustrate Greek private life more completely than any other archæological source of information: peasants and craftsmen, soldiers and traders, housewives, children and their teachers are all portrayed; for Greek athletics and funeral customs they are one of our chief fountains of knowledge.[1] On the other hand the Greek vase painter, like his big brother the sculptor, preferred mythological to historical scenes, and, whichever he illustrated, he allowed free play to his imagination. Some historical value attaches to the paintings on an archaic terra-cotta sarcophagus from Clazomenæ which shows Cimmerian horsemen bearing down upon Greek hoplites[2]; but nothing can be made of the portraits of Alcæus, Sappho, and Anacreon which appear on Greek vases, for these represent nothing but the artist's fancy.[3]

In the second place the distribution of pottery finds is a good index of the volume of Greek industry and the direction of Greek trade. In some instances discoveries of vases have proved the existence of a ceramic industry where none had been suspected. Not the least surprise of the excavations at Sparta was a haul of native Lacon-

---

[1] The funeral "lecythi" of Attica and the "amphoræ" given as prizes to athletes at the Panathenaic games are of particular importance in this respect.

[2] Now in the British Museum.

[3] The question whether the trousered horseman on a vase inscribed "Μιλτιάδης καλός" (now at Oxford) may represent Miltiades himself need not have been raised. The rider's costume is not Scythian but Persian.

ian ware extending from 700 to 350 B.C., and showing considerable artistic merit as late as 550 B.C.[1] But as a rule the most significant finds are of exported pottery, and particularly of wares sent to foreign lands, for these are an excellent index of the direction and quantity of Greek trade. Commercial intercourse with Pharaonic Egypt is plentifully attested by a diverse assortment of Greek ceramic products at the entrepot of Naucratis.[2] A partial Greek penetration of Asia Minor is proved by finds of Rhodian, Corinthian, and especially Attic ware, which competed at Sardes with the vigorous native school of pottery.[3] In S. Russia, and especially in the valleys of the Dnieper and the Bug, Greek importations from the sixth to the fourth century were abundant, and vases of the fifth and fourth centuries were not uncommon along the lower Danube.[4] By the seventh century Greek pottery was making its appearance at Carthage[5] and on the Spanish coast, and at Emporiæ the imports continue right through the fifth century.[6] Vases of the seventh to the fifth century have been found in great abundance in the tombs of the grandees in Etruria and Campania; in Rome the finds of the seventh and sixth century are scanty, those of the fifth century become negligible.

The provenance of the exported ware is a point of no less interest, for it shows where the centres of Greek industry lay and enables us to measure the volume of

[1] J. P. Droop, *B.S.A.* Vols. XIII-XV. For the local Bœotian pottery, see R. M. Burrows and P. N. Ure, *B.S.A.* XIV. p. 226 ff.
[2] H. Prinz, *op. cit.*
[3] W. H. Buckler, *Sardes*, Vol. I.
[4] E. v. Stern, *Klio*, 1909, p. 139 ff.
[5] S. Gsell, *Histoire de l'Afrique du Nord*, Vol. IV. Ch. II.
[6] R. Carpenter, *The Greeks in Spain*, pp. 100-1.

their output. The earlier centres of manufacture were mostly in Asiatic Greece, at Lesbos, Samos, Rhodes, perhaps also Miletus, but the most copious remains are those of the "proto-Corinthian" (see p. 122), Corinthian and Attic fabrics. From *c.* 750 to 650 B.C. proto-Corinthian ware was supreme in eastern and western markets alike; from 650 to 550 B.C. Corinth, which probably had been the carrier for the "proto-Corinthian" potters, displaced the older ware by their own products. By 550 B.C. Attic vases begin to oust the Corinthian products at Naucratis and in the West, and in the fifth century they almost monopolise the Black Sea commerce,[1] which continued flourishing in the fourth century after the decline of the trade to Italy.

[1] E. v. Stern, *op. cit.*

CHAPTER XI

THE documentary evidence for Greek History has not yet been brought together in any single collection of sources. It has to be assembled from literary texts, inscriptions, papyri, etc. For the documents embedded in literary texts no special bibliography is required. The others will be treated in separate sections.

(*A*) INSCRIPTIONS.

(1) *The Corpus.*—The first collection of Greek inscriptions which aimed at complete comprehensiveness was the *Corpus Inscriptionum Græcarum* of August Boeckh, the father of Greek epigraphy. This great work, which took fifty years to complete (1825-77),[1] marked an enormous advance upon its predecessors, which it far surpassed in the number of its texts and in the orderliness of its geographic arrangement. But its standard of accuracy was not sufficiently uniform, and its claim to exhaustiveness was reduced *ad absurdum* by the rapid accumulation of new inscriptions before its completion.

The *C.I.G.* has now been superseded by the *Inscriptiones Græcæ*, which was begun in 1873 under the direction of the Berlin Academy of Sciences and has not

---

[1] Boeckh did not live to see the completion of his work. Vols. III and IV were edited by J. Franz and others.

yet been completed. The new Corpus is planned on the same geographic basis as its predecessor. Vols. I–III are assigned to Attica[1]; IV–VI to Peloponnesus; VII–IX to Central and Northern Greece; X to the Balkans and S. Russia; XI–XIII to the Ægean Islands; XIV to Sicily, Italy, and Western Europe.

The following volumes or parts are still unpublished: VI (Elis and Achæa); VIII (Delphi); X (Balkans and S. Russia); portions of XI (Delos); XII, pt. 4 (Cos); XII, pt. 6 (Chios and Samos); XIII (Crete). Inscriptions from Asia and Africa are not included.

An "Editio Minor" of the Attic inscriptions, in which the facsimile reproductions of the texts are omitted, is being published under the editorship of Hiller von Gärtringen. Up to the present time the following parts have appeared: Vol. I (to 403 B.C.), and parts of Vols. II and III. (1913 ff.)

(2) *Supplements.*— Pending the publication of the unfinished portions of the Corpus, recourse may be had to the following:

Elis: W. Dittenberger and K. Purgold, *Die Inschriften von Olympia.* (Vol. V of Curtius-Adler, *Olympia*; 1896.)

Delphi: C. Wescher and P. Foucart, *Inscriptions recueillies à Delphes* (1863).
Bulletin de correspondance hellénique 1895 ff.
Th. Homolle; *Fouilles de Delphes.* Vol. III, pt. 1 (by E. Bourguet) and pt. 2 (by G. Colin). (1909-13)

---

[1] These originally formed a separate *Corpus Inscriptionum Atticarum* of four volumes. Vol. IV of *C.I.A.*, which contained supplementary texts, is now resolved into *I.G.* I., Supplement, and *I.G.* II. pt. 5.

The articles by H. Pomtow in *Klio*, Vols. XIV–XVIII (1914-22).

S. Russia: B. Latyschev and E. Pridik, *Inscriptiones Antiquæ Oræ Septentrionalis Ponti Euxini Græcæ et Latinæ.* (4 vols., of which No. III, by E. Pridik, contains the inscriptions on amphoræ and titles. Text of Vol. III in Russian. 1885–1917.)

Delos: Bulletin de correspondance hellénique 1882-92, 1902-13.

Cos: W. R. Paton and E. L. Hicks, *The Inscriptions of Cos* (1891).

For the inscriptions of *Asia Minor* the Vienna Academy of Sciences has planned a separate Corpus, named "*Tituli Asiæ Minoris.*" So far only two parts, containing the vernacular and Greek texts from Western Lycia, have appeared (ed. E. Kalinka, 1901-20).

A mass of inscriptions from *Ionia* and *Aeolis* has been published in the following collections:

M. Fränkel, *Die Inschriften von Pergamon* (2 vols.; 1890-95).

Hiller von Gärtringen, *Inschriften von Priene* (1906).

O. Kern, *Die Inschriften von Magnesia-am-Mäander* (1900).

A. Rehm, *Das Delphinion* (Th. Wiegand, *Milet* I, pt 3; 1914).

Vol. III of *The Collection of Ancient Greek Inscriptions in the British Museum* (ed. E. L. Hicks; 1886-90) contains a large number of texts from Priene, Iasus, and Ephesus.

The inscriptions from *Egypt* may be studied in:
W. M. F. Petrie and E. A. Gardner, *Naukratis*, Vol.
II, Ch. VIII.

J. G. Milne, *Catalogue général des antiquités égyptiennes du musée de Caire*, Vol. XVIII (1905).

E. Breccia, *Iscrizioni greche e latine*. ("Catalogue général des antiquités égyptiennes du musée d'Alexandrie"; 1911.)

New texts.—A new annual, the *Supplementum Epigraphicum Græcum* (ed. J. Hondius; Leyden, 1923 ff.) prints each year's fresh texts and gives references to all recent articles connected with epigraphy.

Systematic summaries of new finds and articles on epigraphy have been published by M. N. Tod in the *Journal of Hellenic Studies* (1914-15, 1919, 1921, 1923, 1925), the *Year's Work in Classical Studies* (1906-15), and the *Journal of Egyptian Archæology* (1923 ff.). The occasional articles by Ad. Wilhelm in the *Anzeiger der Akademie der Wissenschaften in Wien*, philosophisch-historische Klasse, and in other periodicals, contain important discussions on new texts, and convincing restorations.

(3) *Selections.*—The supply of these is large and various. A collection of the most important political texts, with brief commentaries, is provided in E. L. Hicks, *Manual of Greek Historical Inscriptions* (1882), and in the second edition of the same work by G. F. Hill (1901). The earlier edition includes texts from the Hellenistic period; the later one omits these, but gives a somewhat fuller selection of texts previous to 323 B.C.

A similar selection of Attic texts, political and other,

is contained in E. S. Roberts and E. A. Gardner, *Introduction to Greek Epigraphy*, Vol. II (1905). The selections by E. Nachmanson, *Historische attische Inschriften* and *Historische griechische Inschriften*, and F. Bleckmann, *Inschriften zur griechischen Staatenkunde* (Vols. CX, CXV, and CXXI, of Lietzmann's *Kleine Texte*; 1913) are on a much smaller scale.

The following works are considerably more extensive, and contain most of the texts of obvious historical importance.

> Ch. Michel, *Recueil d'inscriptions grecques* (1900; first supplement in 1912).
>
> W. Dittenberger, *Sylloge Inscriptionum Græcarum* (third ed., by Hiller v. Gärtringen, in 4 vols., 1915-24).
>
> W. Dittenberger, *Orientis Græci Inscriptiones Selectæ* (2 vols., 1903-5).

In Dittenberger's works the inscriptions are arranged in chronological order, with the exception of Vol. III of the *Sylloge*, which contains a select list of representative texts grouped according to subject-matter. Brief Latin notes are appended. In Michel's selection the texts are classified according to subject, with geographical subdivisions.

A collection of religious texts, complete up to date, and with brief commentaries in Latin, is provided by J. v. Prott and L. Ziehen, *Leges Græcorum Sacræ* (2 vols., 1896-1906).

A small selection of legal texts, with translations and full commentaries, is contained in R. Dareste, B. Haussoullier and Th. Reinach, *Recueil d'inscriptions juridiques grecques* (2 vols., 1890-94).

Many of the historical inscriptions from N.W. Greece, Delphi, Crete, and other regions not yet included in Corpus, will be found in H. Collitz, F. Bechtel and O. Hoffmann, *Sammlung der griechischen Dialekt-Inschriften* (4 vols., 1884-1915).

Facsimiles of archaic Greek texts are reproduced in H. Röhl, *Inscriptiones Græcæ Antiquissimæ*.

(4) *Introductory Handbooks.*—The subject-matter of Greek Inscriptions is reviewed by C. T. Newton in *Essays in Art and Archæology*, ch. 4 (1880). Though no longer up to date, this article is still well worth reading. S. Reinach's *Traité d'épigraphie grecque* contains a translation of Newton's article and a more detailed analysis of the various classes of texts.

W. Larfeld's *Handbuch der griechischen Epigraphik* (2 vols., 1902-7) and *Griechische Epigraphik* (1914) provide highly elaborate analyses. Pt. A of *Griechische Epigraphik* gives an interesting historical survey of Greek epigraphic science.

A brief but bright introduction to epigraphic study will be found in Gercke-Norden's *Einleitung in die Altertumswissenschaft* (third ed.) I pt. 9, pp. 1-26, by Hiller v. Gärtringen.

The history of Greek letter forms may be read in Vol. I of Roberts-Gardner (see p. 130 above), and in A. Kirchhoff, *Studien zur Geschichte des griechischen Alphabets* (fourth ed., 1887). For the orthography and grammar of inscriptions, see K. Meisterhans, *Grammatik der griechischen Inschriften* (third ed., by E. Schwyzer, 1900).

(*B*) Papyri.

(1) *Collections of materials.*—Owing to the rate at which new papyri are still being discovered, the issue of a *Corpus Papyrorum* would at present be premature. The materials therefore of necessity remain scattered among the catalogues of museum and library collections. The editors of these catalogues usually furnish a translation of each text, which in view of the numerous abbreviations used in papyri is an almost essential provision, and short commentaries.

For the study of the Ptolemaic period the most important collections are:

The Petrie Papyri. (*Memoirs of the Royal Irish Academy*, Vols. VIII, IX, XI; 1891–1905. Edited by J. P. Mahaffy and J. G. Smyly.)

The Hibeh Papyri. Ed., B. P. Grenfell and A. S. Hunt. (1906)

The Tebtunis Papyri, Vol. I. Ed. Grenfell, Hunt and Smyly. (1902)

The Revenue Law of Ptolemy Philadelphus, Ed. Grenfell and Mahaffy; full commentary. (1896)

Les Papyrus Lille, Ed. P. Jouguet. (2 vols., 1907–12)

Die Elephantine Papyri, Ed. O. Rubensohn. (1907)

W. Schubart and E. Kühn, *Papyri und Ostraka der Ptolemäerzeit.* ("Ägyptische Urkunden aus den staatlichen Museen zu Berlin," Vol. VI; 1922)

U. Wilcken, *Urkunden der Ptolemäerzeit.* (1922 ff.) This valuable collection, when complete, will comprise all texts previous to the Petrie Papyri. At present 105 texts in three parts have appeared.

Part 2 contains all the documents relating to the "Twins" case.

Papyri Halenses. Vol. I. *Dikaiomata.* (A series of legal documents, edited by F. Bechtel and other scholars of the University of Halle; 1913.) The *London Papyri* (in the British Museum; ed. F. G. Kenyon and H. I. Bell; 5 vols.; 1893-1917), and the famous *Oxyrhynchus Papyri* (ed. Grenfell and Hunt; 16 vols.; 1898-1924) contain few documents of the Ptolemaic period, and of the collection of Michigan little has as yet been published. Stray Ptolemaic texts of interest accur in various minor collections, e.g., *Papyri Grenfell,* Vol. II (1897); *P. Amherst* (1901); *P. Rylands,* Vol. II (1915); *P. Strassburg* (1912-20); *P. Hamburg* (1911-24); *P. Giessen* (1910-12); *P. Freiburg* 1914(ff.) and *Heidelberg* (1914 ff.).

By far the most extensive collection of ostraca is contained in U. Wilcken, *Griechische Ostraka,* Vol. II (1899).

(2) *Supplements.*—Notices of new discoveries will be found in A. S. Hunt's summaries in the *Year's Work in Classical Studies* (1906 ff.), and in H. I. Bell's detailed articles in the *Journal of Egyptian Archæology* (1914 ff.). The chief periodical for papyrology is the *Archiv für Papyrusforschung* (ed. U. Wilcken, 1901 ff.). Articles on papyri are also published in *Ægyptus* (ed. A. Calderini, 1920 ff.).

The "Zeno Correspondence," which constitutes the most important of recent new finds, is being for the most part published in the *Annales du service des antiquités de l'Égypte,* Vol. XVIII (1918 ff.; ed. C. C.

Edgar),and in the *Papiri greci e latini*, Vol. IV (1917 ff.;
ed. G. Vitelli). The Cairo specimens have also begun
to appear in book form. (C. C. Edgar, *The Zeno Papyri*
I. "Catalogue général des antiquités égyptiennes du
musée du Caire, Vol. LXXIX; 1925.)

(3) *Selections:* A few good Ptolemaic documents are
contained in the following:

G. Milligan, *Selections from the Greek Papyri* (1910).

L. Mitteis and U. Wilcken, *Grundzüge und Chrestomathie der Papyruskunde* (texts in 2 vols., 1912).

P. M. Meyer, *Juristische Papyri* (1920).

(4) *Handbooks:*

Mitteis-Wilcken (see above). Introduction to texts
in 2 vols.

W. Schubart, *Einführung in die Papyruskunde* (1918).

W. Schubart, in Gercke-Norden's *Einleitung in die
Altertumswissenschaft* (third ed.) I pt. 9, p. 27-68.

(C) Coins.

(1) *Collections.*—A comprehensive *Corpus Nummorum*
has been projected by the Berlin Academy of Sciences,
but owing to the wide diffusion of the surviving pieces
the completion of this work offers almost insuperable
difficulties. Up to date only three parts relating to
Northern Greece have been published. (*Die antiken
Münzen Nord-Griechenlands*, ed. F. Imhoof-Blumer and
others; 1898 ff.). Of these, part 2 (ed. F. Münzer and
M. Strack; 1912) gives a complete descriptive catalogue
of the Greek towns on the Ægean coast of Thrace.

The principal quarry for numismatic materials consists of the inventories of museum cabinets. Of these

BIBLIOGRAPHY 135

the *Catalogue of Greek Coins in the British Museum* (1873 ff.) is much the most comprehensive. This now includes twenty-seven volumes, in geographical arrangement.

The following catalogues of other British collections are also important:

G. Macdonald, *Greek Coins in the Hunterian Collection* (3 vols.; 1905).

S. W. Grose, *Catalogue of the McLean Collection of Greek Coins*, Vol. I (W. Europe, S. Italy, Sicily; 1923).

Surveys of particular mints are plentiful. The following are only a small selection:

C. T. Seltman, *Athens: Its History and Coinage before the Persian Invasion* (1924).

J. N. Svoronos, *Trésor des monnaies d'Athènes* (to 146 B.C.; 120 plates without text; 1924).

C. T. Seltman, *The Temple Coins of Olympia* (1921).

B. V. Head, *The Coinage of Syracuse* (1874).

W. Giesecke, *Sicilia Numismatica* (1923).

A. J. Evans, *The Horsemen of Tarentum* (1889).

E. T. Newell, *The Seleucid Mint of Antioch* (1918).

J. N. Svoronos, Νομίσματα τοῦ Κράτους τῶν Πτολεμαίων (4 vols., of which no. IV contains a German translation of the Greek text by W. Bardt; 1904-8).

Similar reviews of coin-series, and descriptions of individual new pieces, will be found in the numismatic periodicals. The chief of these are: *The Numismatic Chronicle; The American Journal of Numismatics; Revue numismatique; Numismatische Zeitschrift* (Vienna); *Zeit-*

136 SOURCES OF GREEK HISTORY

schrift für Numismatik (Berlin); *Journal international d'archéologie numismatique* (Athens, 1898-1920).

(2) *Selections.*—For general reference historians will find B. V. Head's *Historia Numorum* (second ed., 1911) admirably adapted to their purpose. In this work the typical pieces of nearly all the Greek mints are briefly described, and illustrations of the most important coins are provided.

A small selection of individual pieces of particular interest, with detailed commentary, is given in G. F. Hill's *Historical Greek Coins* (1906). A larger choice is offered in P. Gardner's *Types of Greek Coins* (with plates and a useful introduction; 1883) and B. V. Head's *Guide to the Principal Gold and Silver Coins of the Ancients in the British Museum* (excellent plates, but no commentary; 1895).

By far the most comprehensive of the selections is E. Babelon's *Traité des monnaies grecques et romaines* (1901 ff.). Of this great work three volumes of descriptive catalogue have appeared, in which the various Greek coin-series down to 306 B.C. are illustrated with some 7,500 specimens. (Text in part 2, nos. 1-3; plates in part 3.)

(3) *Handbooks.*—The best introductory books are G. Macdonald's *Evolution of Coinage* (1916), and *Coin Types* (1905); and the text to P. Gardner's *Types of Greek Coins* (see above). G. F. Hill's *Handbook of Greek and Roman Coins* (1899) is a convenient work of reference.

Individual problems of historical interest are discussed in P. Gardner's *History of Ancient Coinage*, B.C. 700-300 (1918), and in Th. Reinach's *L'Histoire par les mon-*

naies (1902). Part I of Babelon's work discusses at length the characteristics of ancient coinage (3 vols., 1901 ff.).

(*D*) Unwritten Documents.

For a brief general survey, see E. A. Gardner, in D. G. Hogarth, *Authority and Archæology*, Pt. 2, Ch. III (second ed., 1899).

(1) *Architectural remains.*—Our chief source of information consists in the reports of excavations. These are usually presented in provisional articles in the leading archæological periodicals previous to their publication (often *longo intervallo*) in book form.

The periodicals which chiefly require consultation are: *The Journal of Hellenic Studies; The Annual of the British School at Athens; The American Journal of Archæology; Bulletin de correspondance hellénique; Mitteilungen des deutschen archäologischen Instituts zu Athen; Jahrbuch des deutschen archäologischen Instituts; Jahreshefte des österreichischen archäologischen Instituts in Wien; Notizie degli Scavi di Antichita; Πρακτικὰ τῆς ἐν Ἀθήναις Ἀρχαιολογικῆς Ἑταιρείας.*

Of the definitive reports of excavations, the following are among the most important:

E. Gabrici, *Cuma.* (Monumenti Antichi. Reale Accademia dei Lincei; 1913 ff.)

Th. Homolle, etc., *Exploration archéologique de Delos* (1909 ff.).

Th. Homolle, etc., *Fouilles de Delphes* (1902 ff.).

D. G. Hogarth, *The Excavations at Ephesus* (1908).

O. Benndorf, etc., *Forschungen in Ephesus* (1906 ff.).

138   SOURCES OF GREEK HISTORY

P. Cavvadias, Τὸ 'Ιερὸν τοῦ 'Ασκληπιοῦ ἐν 'Επιδαύρῳ (1900).
P. Orsi, *Gela* (1906).
C. Walston, etc., *The Argive Heræum* (1902).
C. Humann, *Magnesia-am-Mäander* (1904).
E. A. Gardner, etc., *Megalopolis*. (*Journal of Hellanic Studies*, Supplement I; 1892.)
Th. Wiegand, etc., *Milet* (1906 ff.).
W. M. F. Petrie and E. A. Gardner, *Naukratis* (1886-8).
E. Curtius, etc., *Olympia* (1890-97).
A. Conze, etc., *Altertümer von Pergamon* (1885-1923).
Th. Wiegand and H. Schrader, *Priene* (1904).
Hiller von Gärtringen, etc., *Thera* (1899-1909).

No definitive account of the excavations at Sparta has yet appeared, and the final reports on Delos and Delphi are far from complete. For Sparta, see *B.S.A.*, Vol. XII (1905) ff.; for Delos, *B.C.H.* 1877-91, 1902 ff.; for Delphi, *B.C.H.* 1881 ff., and the articles by H. Pomtow in *Klio* 1907-9, 1912-13.

Discussions of the chief results of excavation will be found in:

E. A. Gardner, *Ancient Athens* (1902).
M. L. d'Ooge, *The Acropolis of Athens* (1908).
F. Poulsen, *Delphi* (transl. by G. C. Richards, 1920).
M. Collignon, *Pergame* (1900).
P. Gardner, *New Chapters in Greek History* (chs. on Athens, Epidaurus, Naucratis, Olympia; 1892).
Ch. Diehl, *Excursions in Greece* (transl. by E. Perkins, 1893: chs. on Athens, Delos, Epidaurus, Olympia).

For a brief survey of recent excavations *cf.* F. H. Marshall, *Discoveries in Greek Lands* (1920).

(2) *Sculpture.*—A critical discussion of extant Greek portraits is given in J. J. Bernoulli, *Griechische Ikonographie* (1901). For a treatise on Greek sculpture, including the chief historical pieces, see E. A. Gardner, *Handbook of Greek Sculpture* (second ed., 1905).

(3) *Pottery.*—A representative collection of ceramic products of all ancient peoples, the *Corpus Vasorum*, has been planned by the Union académique internationale under the direction of E. Pottier (1923 ff.). Of the eight regional groups in this collection, Greece makes up one. The four instalments hitherto published contain miscellaneous specimens from different countries, but all the Greek vases are grouped together on the same plate.

The catalogues of the principal museums are still the chief storehouse of information on ceramic ware. These include the *British Museum Catalogue of Pottery* (H. B. Walters and C. H. Smith; 1893-1912); *Catalogue of the Greek and Etruscan Vases in the British Museum*, I Pt. I (E. J. Forsdyke, 1925); do. of *Terracottas* (H. B. Walters, 1903); *The Hope Vases* (E. M. W. Tillyard; 1923); and the Catalogues of the Louvre and New York Museum.

Complete lists of vases with artists' signatures are contained in J. C. Hoppin's *Handbook of Black-Figure Vases* (1914); *Handbook of Red-Figure Vases* (1918-9).

Many important clues as to the direction and volume of the trade in pottery are contained in H. Prinz, *Funde aus Naukratis* (*Klio*, Beiheft VII, 1908).

For a general account of Greek ceramics, see H. B. Walters, *Handbook of Greek Pottery* (2 vols., 1905).

(4) *Other small objects.*—The chief sources of information are the museum catalogues, e.g., the *British Museum Catalogue of Bronzes* (H. B. Walters, 1898); of *Jewellery* (F. H. Marshall, 1911); of *Engraved Gems* (A. S. Murray, 1888).